COLLINS GEM GUIDE

GARDEN FLOWERS

Text by Christopher Grey-Wilson
Illustrations by Victoria Goaman

D0187877

HarperCollinsPublishers

HarperCollins Publishers
PO Box, Glasgow G4 0NB

First published 1986

Reprint 9 8 7 6 5

ISBN 0 00 458823 1

Printed in Great Britain by
HarperCollins Manufacturing, Glasgow

Contents

Introduction

The countless numbers of different flowers grown in gardens can be enjoyed by everyone. Some have been developed from native species but the origins of the majority are scattered across the face of the globe. Selection from the many types can provide colour throughout the year and a continuous tapestry of interest.

This volume concentrates on the border plants which are so important in gardens. A whole host of common and less common species are included to illustrate the very wide range available to the gardener, so that you will be able to identify flowers you see and choose plants you would like to grow. Trees, shrubs and most alpine plants have been omitted; there simply would not be room for them in a book this size.

Choosing plants or selecting seeds, and planning their planting, can be a pleasant winter occupation, followed, as the seasons advance, by the excitement of the flowers coming into bloom.

Identifying garden flowers can prove very bothersome because of the great variety of plants cultivated. Further complication is added by the many selected forms and hybrids which have often been given cultivar names, for example *Geranium* 'Johnson's Blue'. These are usually particularly fine forms and

5

some are mentioned at the end of plant descriptions, though many others will be available than can be listed here.

It is fairly easy for anyone who knows just a little about flowers to place most plants at least in a group – Primroses, Gentians, Geraniums and so on. It is then a matter of finding these in the text and trying to match the living plant against the illustration. But remember, this book cannot include every garden plant. Supplement it by keeping a selection of illustrated catalogues from nurseries and seedsmen to give you pictures of even more forms and to help you ascertain the names of the many varieties nurserymen have developed.

Record the names of new plants in the garden, because they are easily forgotten. Tag plants with suitable labels, or write the names down in a log book or diary, with an indication of their appearance and location.

Arrangement in the text All the plants are arranged according to their botanical families, so that those with similar characteristics come close together. Thus all daisies and thistle-like plants which belong to the family Compositae (Daisy Family) are grouped together. Likewise, the Anemones, Buttercups and the Marsh Marigold, which belong to the Ranunculaceae (Buttercup Family) also come close together in the text.

When several species are described within a genus, the first word of the scientific name is usually abbreviated to its initial letter for second and subsequent species, for example, *G. sanguineum* for *Geranium sanguineum*. Illustrations are identified by bold numbers (**1**) which also appear after their names in the text. Area of origin and flowering times are given at the end of each description. Where no specific information is given it will be the same as the preceding species or variety.

Codes used in the text In order to include as much information as possible the following information has been coded:

ASPECT Some plants require full sun, others prefer shade or half-shade, as shown below.

- ☼ full sun
- ◒ half shade
- ● full shade
- △ flowers especially good for cutting
- ★ flowers or fruits good for drying for decoration

PLANT TYPES are indicated in two ways, according to both habit and hardiness.

- A annual, plants that are grown from seed, flower, seed and die all in the same year.
- B biennial, plants that germinate in the first year but do not flower until the second. Like annuals, biennials die after flowering, having first set seed.
- P perennial, plants that flower year after year and are mostly long-lived. Most perennials flower for the first time in their second season, although some may take longer.
- H plants that are hardy and frost tolerant.
- HH plants that are half-hardy and not reliably frost hardy.
- T particularly tender subjects, that will quickly succumb to low temperatures, not necessarily frost and chill winds.

Annuals can thus be classified as hard HA, half-hardy HHA or tender TA. The same applies to both biennials and perennials.

Cultivation

Preparing the soil Before anything is planted the soil should be carefully prepared. New ground is best if double-dug, removing all perennial weeds at the same time. Manure or compost can be incorporated into the soil, placing it at the base of each trench before the next spit is turned over.

Well-worked ground may only require a light forking over and the application of a general fertilizer. Ground is best raked level before any sowing or planting is undertaken and it is generally helpful to mark out the area with canes and string so that plants can be properly balanced in the border. Draw up a plan of plants and their positions on paper to make it easier to design the layout of beds and borders.

Annuals Few plants can beat annuals for a quick and colourful display. Annual borders were very popular a few years ago and are once again coming into favour. Annuals are also ideal as gap fillers in the herbaceous border, or for filling the space between shrubs. Many, such as Petunias and Lobelia, are ideal for large pots and tubs in patio gardens.

Half-hardy and tender annuals are usually sown in March in heated frames and greenhouses in temperatures of 16-18°C. When large enough to handle, the seedlings should be pricked out into boxes or pans. In May and early June plants should be gradually hardened off for planting out when all danger of late frosts has passed.

Hardy annuals are generally sown where they are to flower. The ground design can be marked out with a pointed stick or with lines of silver sand. Seed can be broadcast or sown in parallel drills 10-12cm apart, and lightly covered. Seedlings will need vigorous thinning, otherwise the resultant plants will be spindly and poorly flowered. When in doubt always follow the instructions on the seed packet. Hardy annuals can be sown from March until May for the summer, or alternatively many can be sown in early September for an early show the following year.

Perennials The herbaceous border is an attractive feature in any garden, but needs careful planning for the best results, with attention given to colour and height, as well as the form of its various components. Herbaceous perennials generally look best when planted in groups of at least three plants. The basic principal is to grade the heights so that the tallest varieties are at the back of the border. Such borders often require a good deal of attention to keep them in good condition and many gardeners prefer the 'island bed' for which shorter, mostly self-supporting, varieties are selected. Island beds can take a formal or informal shape, the tallest plants being placed towards the centre.

Herbaceous perennials can be increased by dividing the parent clumps. This is usually done every three or four years. Large clumps can be teased apart using two garden forks back-to-back and levering them against one another. Alternatively, they can be grown from seed. Seedlings can be planted out in lines during the first season in an odd corner of the garden, before they are introduced to their flowering positions. Most will flower in their second season.

Half-hardy perennials will need some protection, especially during severe winter weather. A cloche or a guard of straw, bracken or sacking may be all that is required. Alternatively, plants can be overwintered in a frame or cold greenhouse. In all but the mildest districts, tender perennials will have to be dug up and removed to a frost-free place to overwinter or cuttings taken and grown indoors for the next year.

Biennials can be treated in much the same way as perennials. Such types as Sweet Williams and Foxgloves are best sown in the spring or early summer. Young plants can be lined out during the summer in some spare ground. In the autumn they can be transferred to their flowering positions.

Staking Care in staking taller annuals and perennials with 'pea sticks' or canes can make all the difference to the look of the flower border. Most of the taller annuals and perennials, except those with strong stiff growth, will benefit from being staked. Stakes should be placed around the plants well in advance of flowering, so that they are concealed by the time the plants come into flower. Branched pea-sticks are ideal or canes can be used and plants loosely tied with soft string, raffia or commercially produced ties.

Collecting your own seed It is often quite easy to save your own seeds, especially those of annual species. Seed of many varieties will reproduce 'true to character,' though those of some named cultivars and hybrids will not come true. Seedpods, fruits or heads should be gathered as they ripen and placed in paper bags to hold the escaping seeds. These should be kept in a sunny dry place. Most seeds are best dried as quickly as possible in a dry, airy but not hot, place and then separated from the fruit or capsule remains. They can then be sealed in envelopes until required – make sure that each packet is carefully marked with the name of the species or variety, as well as the date

– and stored in a cool dry place. Most seeds are best kept to be sown in the following spring, however, those of certain types, especially Primroses, Blue Poppies and Gentians are short-lived and quickly lose their capacity to germinate. Such seeds are best sown the moment they are ripe.

Cutting flowers is best done in the early morning or during the evening. At other times, especially during hot summer weather, flowers may be partially wilted. Cut in such a state, their life in water will be reduced. Most flowers benefit from a three or four hour soak in a deep bucket of water before they are used for arrangements. Annual and perennial border plants provide some of the very best flowers for cutting.

Drying flowers Flowers suitable for drying, such as Onion heads, Yarrow and Everlasting Flowers, can be readily dried for winter decoration and can be highly ornamental. Flowers are best cut when fully developed, fruitheads as they begin to dry out. They should be cut with a good length of stem. Excess leaves can be stripped off, then the stems tied into small bunches. These are then hung upside down in a warm airy place to dry.

1

ACANTHUS FAMILY **Acanthus** are robust, creeping, sometimes invasive, perennials making bold groups with their handsome cut leaves and striking spiny spikes of flowers. The leaf pattern of *A. mollis* HP was used by the ancient Greeks on Corinthian columns. It is a vigorous plant growing to 1m or more, with close-set bronzy-purple flowers having a contrasting white lip. *A. spinosus* (**1**) HP has more sharply cut leaves and pale mauve and purple flowers. Both come from S. Europe and succeed on most average garden soils. Jul.-Sept. ☼☕★

ICE PLANT FAMILY A family of fleshy plants with brightly coloured daisy-like flowers. Most come from southern Africa and include the curious 'Living Stones' or *Lithops*. **Ice Plant** *Cryophytum crystallinum* (**2**) HHA is a strange prostrate annual with its stems and tongue-like leaves covered in a crystalline coat. The small yellowish or pinkish flowers are of little significance. **Livingstone Daisy** *Dorotheanthus bellidiflorus* (= *Mesembryanthemum criniflorum*) (**3**) HHA is altogether more spectacular, a prostrate annual up to 30cm across with reddish stems and crystalline encrusted leaves. The 2.5-4cm flowers come in a wide range of colours: pink, red, apricot, purple or white, often with a contrasting 'eye.' Both require a sunny position for the flowers to open. Jul.-Sept. ☼

2

3

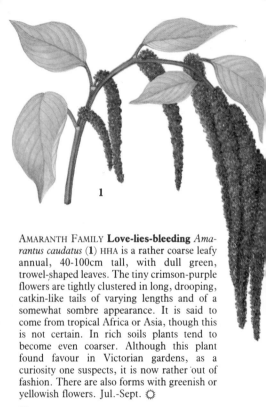

1

AMARANTH FAMILY **Love-lies-bleeding** *Amarantus caudatus* (**1**) HHA is a rather coarse leafy annual, 40-100cm tall, with dull green, trowel-shaped leaves. The tiny crimson-purple flowers are tightly clustered in long, drooping, catkin-like tails of varying lengths and of a somewhat sombre appearance. It is said to come from tropical Africa or Asia, though this is not certain. In rich soils plants tend to become even coarser. Although this plant found favour in Victorian gardens, as a curiosity one suspects, it is now rather out of fashion. There are also forms with greenish or yellowish flowers. Jul.-Sept. ☼

PERIWINKLE FAMILY Periwinkles are superb subjects for dry bare corners of the garden, especially below trees. All the species are rather rampant and are best trimmed back immediately after flowering. **Greater Periwinkle** *Vinca major* (**3**) HP is the coarsest with shiny green leaves and blue flowers, 35-50mm across. 'Variegata' – leaves variegated with cream. Europe. Mar.-Jun. ☼● **Lesser Periwinkle** *V. minor* (**2**) HP is smaller and neater with deep green leaves and bright blue flowers, seldom more than 25mm across. Europe. Mar.-May. ☼ 'Atropurpurea' - purplish flowers; 'Bowles Variety' - a more compact form; 'Jekyll's White' - white flowers.

DAFFODIL FAMILY **Daffodils and Narcissi** are probably more widely grown than any other bulbous plant. A bewildering array of cultivars exist and bulb catalogues should be consulted when making a selection. Most of the large trumpet daffodils are derived from the Wild Daffodil, *Narcissus pseudonarcissus*, which exists in numerous forms in the wild. Cultivars such as 'King Alfred'(**2**) and 'Mount Hood' (**3**) are typical of these. Crosses with the Poet's Narcissus, *N. poeticus*, have given rise to the small cup forms such as 'Scarlet Elegance'(**5**). Today there is a trend toward the smaller, more refined blooms, often with swept-back petals which are inherited from such alpine species as *N. cyclamineus* and *N. triandrus*, natives of Spain. These are more expensive to buy but good examples are 'Dove Wings', 'Thalia' (**6**) 'February Gold'(**1**) and 'Barrett-Browning' (**4**).

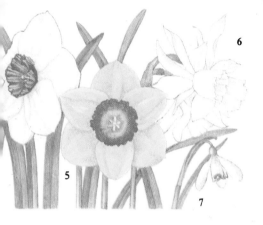

Most Daffodils and Narcissi thrive in ordinary garden soil, providing that it is well-drained. They are ideal for naturalizing amongst trees or in grass, or simply as groups to enliven borders early in the year. All of them are absolutely hardy. Feb.-May. ☼☷△

Snowdrop *Galanthus nivalis* (**7**) is a great favourite of cottage gardeners. There are many forms and numerous named cultivars, but the simplicity of the wild form, with its drooping white blooms, is hard to beat. Plants are best in clumps and these need to be divided every three or four years, immediately after flowering. Originated in C. & E. Europe. Feb.-Apr. ☼☷△ There is also a widely grown double variety, 'Flore Plena'. Both single and double forms will seed themselves around, once established.

19

MILKWEED FAMILY A primarily tropical family which contains the exotic genus *Hoya*, several species of which make fine pot plants. The **Milkweed** or **Butterfly Weed** *Asclepias tuberosa* HHP is an erect hairy plant, up to 50cm tall, with oblong leaves which clasp the stem. The striking bunches of *Hoya*-like flowers are borne on short stalks and are orange-yellow with a deep orange-red centre or 'corona'. In its native habitat in North America the flowers are visited by the beautiful Monarch butterflies. A plant well deserving to be more widely grown, although only succeeding in sheltered warm gardens. Aug.-Oct. ☼ The related *A. curassavica* (**1**) TP, with more pointed leaves and vivid red flowers, can be grown as a half-hardy annual.

1

BUSY-LIZZY FAMILY The explosive fruits of *Impatiens* are a constant delight to children. Most species have a fleshy appearance with bright glistening flowers. **Garden Balsam** *I.balsamina* HHA, from tropical Asia, grows 20-50cm tall with narrow leaves. The double or 'Camellia-flowered' strains are the finest, in shades of pink and red, mauve or white. Jun.-Aug. ☼ **Himalayan Balsam** *I. glandulifera* (**3**) HA is well known but too invasive for all but the wild garden. Bumble bees love it. Jul.-Sept. ❂ *I. balfourii* (**2**) HA from Kashmir is far more suitable, growing to 50cm and flowering profusely. Jul.-Oct. ☼❂●

1

2

BARBERRY FAMILY **Epimediums** HP are an
excellent group of tolerant plants succeeding
in a wide variety of soils, including poor dry
soils in shaded situations. They are tufted
perennials with modest four-parted flowers
and pretty, divided foliage, often good for
autumn colour. *E. pinnatum*, from W. Asia,
has handsome prickly-edged leaves and long
racemes of yellow flowers. 'Rose Queen' = *E.
grandiflorum* 'Rose Queen' (**1**) is the best form.
E. x *warleyense* is a robust plant with coppery
flowers (**2**). *E.* x *youngianum* is the finest of all
with its dainty pure white flowers and
handsome foliage. There is a good pink form

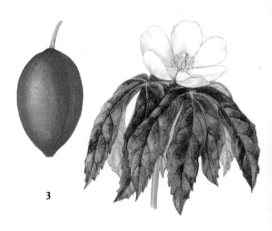

3

-'Roseum'. All those mentioned are hardy perennials and make good ground cover subjects, 20-30cm tall. Apr.-May. ☼● **Podophyllum** *P. emodi* (**3**) is a handsome Himalayan plant relishing moist leafy soils where it will creep eventually, though slow to establish. In the spring the stiff, fleshy shoots bear two reflexed leaves on each side of a white or pale pink, poppy-like flower, 3-5cm across. The striking bronzy leaves, lobed and conspicuously veined, expand as the flowers fade. The plum-like fruit droops below the foliage, green at first, but red and edible when ripe. 'Majus' is a particularly fine form. Apr.-May. ☼●

1

BIGNONIA FAMILY This primarily tropical family includes many rampant climbers and trees. *Cobaea* and *Eccremocarpus* are widely grown climbers, but only the herbaceous *Incarvillea* can be said to be fully hardy in our gardens. *I. delavayi* (**1**) HP has an exotic appearance, indeed some may think too exotic for a place in their borders. It is an erect plant 30-50cm tall with dull-green pinnate leaves. The splendid bold trumpet flowers are deep pink with a pale yellow throat, each 5-6.5cm long and borne in small clusters on long stout scapes. A native of China, requiring well-drained soils. Jun.-Jul. ☼

BORAGE FAMILY A very large family, primarily from temperate regions, with flowers borne in distinct coils or cymes and much loved by bees. **Anchusa** *A. italica* HP is a robust, erect, very bristly plant up to 120cm tall. The numerous flowers are relatively large and a glorious rich deep blue. Easy to grow in most average soils, although it usually requires staking. Mediterranean. May-Jul. ☼ There are a number of fine cultivars which often seed about, once established, including: 'Dropmore' - 90cm, pale blue'; 'Little John' - 45cm, bright blue; 'Loddon Royalist' (**2**) - 90cm, rich blue, perhaps finest of all.

2

BORAGE FAMILY (contd) **Blue-eyed Mary** *Omphalodes verna* (**1**) HP, a low creeping carpeter, up to 10cm high, is ideal for ground cover, with delicate sprays of bright sky-blue flowers of 'forget-me-not type'. C. Europe. Mar.-May. ☾● 'Alba' has white flowers, but is generally less effective. *O. cappadocica* (**2**) is very much finer and less invasive, up to 15cm tall, with tufts of large green, often bronzed, ribbed leaves and cymes of relatively large, intensely bright blue flowers. W. Asia. Apr.-Jun. ☾ 'Anthea Bloom' has sky-blue flowers. Both will succeed on ordinary moist soils. **Borage** *Borage officinalis* (**3**) HA/HB is a popular herb, widely naturalized in Europe. Plants are erect with bristly, rather brittle, much-branched stems and

3

4

large oblong basal leaves. The numerous drooping star-shaped flowers are bright blue with a cone of stamens protruding below. An easy and long-cultivated species, often seeding around freely. The leaves and flowers are often added as a flavouring to cooling drinks. E. Mediterranean. Jun.-Sept. ☼☂ **Echium** or **Bugloss** *E. platagineum* (**4**) HA/HB is an erect, rather striking plant, up to 80cm tall, with narrow pointed basal leaves and large pyramidal clusters of flowers. These are rather irregular with a short tube, dark blue with protruding stamens. Nurserymen supply both pink and blue forms. Mediterranean and W. Europe. Jul.-Sept. ☼

1

2

BORAGE FAMILY (contd) **Chinese Forget-me-not**
Cynoglossum amabile (**1**) HB is an erect plant, growing
to 60cm or more, with velvety leaves and branched
stems of lovely cobalt-blue flowers. Easy to grow in
moist open situations and often seeding freely once
established. W. China. Jul.-Aug. ☼◑ **Brunnera** *B.
macrophylla* (**2**), a coarse tufted plant, up to 45cm tall,
bearing numerous small flowers. Excellent ground
cover in dry shaded areas. C. Asia. Apr.-Jun. ☼◑●
'Variegata' has leaves blotched with cream. **Comfreys**
Symphytum The Common Comfrey *S. officinalis* is a

well-known European native, though too gross for the average garden. *S. caucasium* (**3**) HP is perhaps the finest, forming large spreading tufts up to 90cm tall with large grey-green leaves and sprays of bright blue flowers which are most effective *en masse*. Caucasus. Apr.-Jun. and later. ☘● *S. grandiflorum* HP, from the same region, forms low creeping mats carrying loose clusters of cream flowers, often red in bud. Good ground cover. Mar.-May. ☘● *S. orientale* (**4**) HP is widely grown, up to 50cm tall, with heart-shaped leaves and congested clusters of china blue or white flowers. Excellent for naturalizing. Turkey. Apr.-May. ☘ None of these should be planted where they are likely to swamp less robust neighbours.

3

4

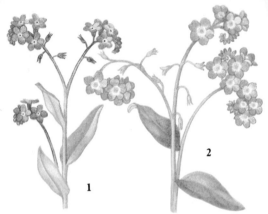

1

2

BORAGE FAMILY **Forget-me-nots** *Myosotis* The Common Forget-me-not (**1**) of gardens belongs to one of two species, *M. sylvatica* HB and *M. dissitiflora* HB, which are difficult to tell apart. Both have branched, 20cm stems bearing numerous small bright blue, occasionally pink or white, flowers. The former is a British native, the latter probably from Switzerland. Mar.-Jun. ☼☽ Dwarf or compact forms such as 'Blue Ball' and 'Victoria' are worth seeking out. *M. scorpioides* (**2**)HP is a finer plant, laxer in habit, with a creeping stock, paler foliage and relatively large Cambridge-blue flowers. Requires moist soils. Europe. May-Jun. ☼☽ **Lungworts** *Pulmonaria*, are widely grown, dual-purpose, tufted plants which have attractive flowers and rather handsome, often blotched, foliage. *P. angustifolia* (**3**) HP has narrow spear-shaped unspotted leaves and stems up to 20cm tall. The flowers are relatively large, red in bud but opening violet-blue. Europe. Mar.-Apr. ☼☽● 'Azurea' - the finest form. *P. mollis* HP has unspotted leaves and loose clusters of bright red flowers. C. & S.E. Europe. Feb.-Apr. ☽ *P. saccharata* (**4**) HP is perhaps the best species for our gardens, 25cm tall, with broad elliptical spotted leaves. The flowers commence pink or red but eventually turn violet-blue. Italy. Mar.-May. ☼☽ 'Pink Dawn' - pink flowers; 'Bowles Red' - striking red flowers; 'Highdown' - rich blue. *P. officinalis* HP is similar but coarser. N. & C. Europe. Mar.-May. ☼☽ All are ideal for edging borders or for ground cover.

3

4

BORAGE FAMILY (contd) **Virginian Cowslip** *Mertensia virginica* (**1**) HP is one of the most aristocratic members of the family, with loose erect stems 30-60cm tall. The fleshy, oblong leaves are grey-green and contrast with the drooping clusters of sky-blue, bell-shaped flowers. A charming plant for moist cool places, but beware - slugs and snails relish its succulent stems and leaves. N. America. Apr.-May. ☽● **Lithospermum** *L. diffusum* (**2**) HP is really a subshrub, half-trailing, up to 25cm tall with narrow oblong bristly leaves and small clusters of striking, deep blue flowers. Easy to grow but resenting heavy calcareous soils, so requiring leafy and peaty soils. Mediterranean. May-Jul. ☼ Selected forms, such as 'Heavenly Blue' and 'Grace Ward' are splendid and have larger flowers.

BELLFLOWER FAMILY An extensive family containing many popular garden plants, though mostly belonging to two genera, *Campanula* and *Lobelia*. Except for the choice little alpine species, most will succeed on very ordinary soils. **Clustered Bellflower** *Campanula glomerata* (**3**) HP is a spreading, often rampant, plant, 30-60cm tall with coarse leafy stems topped by a cluster of deep violet-blue flowers. Europe & Asia. May-Aug. ☼☁ 'Joan Elliot' - violet flowers △; 'Nana Alba' - white flowers. *C. lactiflora* (**4**) HP is more robust, up to 1.5m tall with broad loose panicles of powder-blue bells. Caucasus. Jul.-Aug. ☼☁△

3

4

1

2

BELLFLOWER FAMILY (contd) **Chimney Bellflower**
Campanula pyramidalis (**1**) HP is a stiff giant, growing
to 2m, with shiny heart-shaped leaves and large
panicles of pale blue or white bells. Often grown as a
biennal and requiring more shelter and moisture than
its cousins. Italy and the Balkans. July-Aug. ☼ *C.
latifolia* is better known, reaching 1m tall, and
bearing graceful racemes of half-nodding pale blue or
white bells. A native species. Jun.-Jul. *C. alliarifolia*
HP is larger and coarser with deep blue flowers. *C.
persicifolia* (**2**) HP is a charming and useful plant, often
seen in old cottage gardens. The slender stems may
reach 1m tall with narrow deep green leaves and

3

broad horizontal or upright blue or white bells. There are both single- and double-flowered forms. S. Europe. Jun.-Aug. ☼☺△ **Canterbury Bell** C. *media* (**3**) HB, like the Stock and Sweet William, has long been a favourite cottage garden plant, though less seen today than formerly. However, there are few bolder plants in our gardens. In the first year plants form a coarse rosette of bristly leaves. In the second year the stem elongates to 60-80cm, bearing a broad pyramid of large bells in shades of blue, violet, pink or white. S. Europe. Jun.-Jul. ☼☺ There are double-flowered forms but the finest and most sought-after are the 'Cup and Saucer' types (var. *calycantha*) in which the bell (cup) is surrounded by a similarly coloured calyx (the saucer).

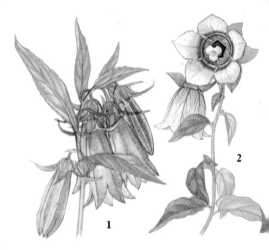

1

2

BELLFLOWER FAMILY (contd) *Campanula* x *bourgatii* (**1**) HP is a superb and unusual hybrid forming clumps with pale green leaves and slender stems up to 60cm long. The large nodding bells are an enticing grey-blue, almost opaque and quite exquisite. **Codonopsis** are superficially like the Bellflowers, the flowers often beautifully patterned inside, but do not get too close for most have an evil smell. *C. clematidea* (**2**) HP forms tangled mats, up to 40cm tall, with slender branched stems bearing small grey-green, heart-shaped leaves and subtle grey-blue broad bells. Himalaya. June-July. ☼☂ *C. ovata* HP is finer,

3

similar but smaller, with delightful china-blue flowers. W. Himalaya. Jun.-Jul. ☼☽ **Balloon Flower** *Platycodon grandiflorum* (**3**) HP is a real gem which deserves to be far more widely grown. The tuberous rootstock supports a number of erect stems 40-60cm tall, with broad elliptic leaves. The large, broad bellflowers are solitary or several together, blue, occasionally pink or white. The flower buds are inflated, hence the common name. Will succeed on any good soil. N. & E. Asia. Jun.-Aug. ☼ Var. *mariesii* is a more compact form. 'Snowflake' - has semi-double white flowers.

BELLFLOWER FAMILY (contd) *Lobelia erinus* (**2**) HHP is one of the most useful of summer bedding plants, easy to grow and very floriferous. The bush types are 7-15cm tall, with flowers in all shades of blue, violet, purple, red or white. S. Africa Jun.-Sept. ☼☽ 'Cambridge-Blue', 'Crystal Palace', 'Crimson Gem' and 'Port Wine' are fine cultivars. **Cardinal Flower** *L. cardinalis* TP is a handsome plant up to 1m tall with narrow green leaves and spikes of fiery scarlet flowers. Moist soils. N. America. Aug.-Sept. ☽ *L.*

splendens (**1**) TP, often sold under the previous name, is similar but with bronzy-purple leaves.

CAPER FAMILY This family contains many species from tropical regions. **Spider Flower** *Cleome (= Gynandropsis) speciosa* (**3**) HHA is a stout herb 90-120cm tall, with hairy stems and hand-like leaves. The large spidery flowers are borne in elegant erect racemes. They are rose-pink or white with long purplish stamens. Easy to grow, but best in hot sunny summers. C. America. Aug.-Sept. ☼

3

CATCHFLY FAMILY A large and important temperate family with many fine species cultivated in our gardens. **Corncockle** *Agrostemma githago* (**1**) HA is now a rare inhabitant of our 'cornfields'. 'Milas' is a super form, 60-70cm tall, with silky branched stems and large cerise-pink flowers. Jul.-Aug. ☼ **Jerusalem Cross** *Lychnis chalcedonicum* (**2**) HP is a stiff hairy plant, up to 1m tall, with leafy stems and large flat clusters of vivid scarlet flowers. E. USSR. Jun.-Aug. ☼△ **Rose Campion** *L. coronaria* (**3**) HB is a tufted plant, 30-90cm tall, with coarse woolly leaves and

4

5

solitary cerise-crimson or white flowers. An old cottage garden plant. C. & S. Europe. Jun.-Sept. ☼☽ **Flower of Jove** L. *flos-jovis* (**5**) HP is similar but shorter, with rose-pink flowers in small tight clusters. C. & S. Europe. Jun.-Jul. ☼ **Sticky Catchfly** L. *viscaria* (**4**) HP is another favourite cottage plant, with sticky stems up to 50cm tall. Flowers in small branched clusters, carmine-pink. C. Europe. Jun.-Jul. ☼ 'Alba' - white flowers; 'Splendens Plena' - a fine form with double cerise flowers.

CATCHFLY FAMILY (contd) Pinks and Carnations have been developed from several species of *Dianthus*, though most notably *D. plumarius* and *D. sinensis*. **Garden Pink** *D. plumarius* HP has given rise to a number of fine races, mostly with double, fringed flowers and with a typical clove-fragrance. Most form compact cushions of grey-green slender leaves with flowering stems up to 25cm tall. Jun.-Aug. ☼△ There are numerous varieties, both old and new. 'Miss Sinkins' (**1**) - double white, is a well-known old favourite; 'Excelsior' - a pink form of the previous. Others include 'Doris' - pink with a deeper centre; 'Emperor'; - double red; 'Paddington' - pale pink flecked crimson; 'Sam Barlow' - pink and white.

Chinese Pink *D. sinensis* HA is a straggling plant 15-35cm tall, with broad coarse green leaves and large single, fringed flowers in white, pink, magenta or purple. Jun.-Sept. ☼ **Carnation** *D. caryophyllus* forms have been cultivated for many centuries. There are many varieties cultivated under glass for the florist trade. The famous 'Allwoodii' carnations are selected crosses with *D. plumarius* cultivars. Good border varieties include 'All Spice' (**5**), 'Gran's Favourite' (**4**) and 'Laced Joy' (**3**). **Maiden Pink** *D. deltoides* (**2**)HP is a loose mat-forming plant with small dull- or purplish-green leaves and slender stems 15-20cm long, carrying small flowers in shades of crimson, pink or white and often speckled. A good path edger. W. Europe. Jun.-Aug. ☼ 'Flashing Light' - salmon scarlet; 'Samos' - carmine.

CATCHFLY FAMILY (contd) **Gypsophila** is well-known, easy to grow and fine for cutting. *G. paniculata* HP is a robust plant with thick thong-like roots, slender stems and narrow grey-green leaves, forming a dense bush up to 90cm tall. The tiny white or pale pink flowers are borne in a misty profusion of great elegance. S. Europe. Jun.-Sept. ☼☻△ 'Bristol Fairy' - double-white, the finest; 'Flamingo' - pink, double' 'Rosy Veil' (**2**) - shell-pink, double, only 25cm tall. **Annual Gypsophila** *G. elegans* (**1**) HA, a slender wiry plant up to 45cm tall with greyish leaves and numerous pink or white flowers. W. Asia. Jul.-Aug. ☼△ **Snow in Summer** *Cerastium tomentosum* (**3**) HP There are gardeners who never allow this plant past the front gate, yet if it is given the right position, such as a dry sunny bank, driveway or the edge of a retaining wall, this 'everyday plant' can look most effective. It is, however, rather invasive, forming spreading mats of silvery-white narrow leaves. The slender branched stems bear small pure white flowers with typical notched petals. Plants can be trimmed back after flowering to keep them in check. Plants can be easily increased, simply by breaking up the parent plant into small, rooted pieces. A useful subject for smothering weeds. Europe. May-Jul. ☼

3

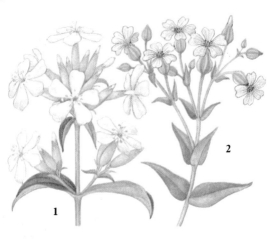

CATCHFLY FAMILY **Soapwort or Bouncing Bet**
Saponaria officinalis (**1**)HP, a long-cultivated, favourite cottage garden plant, is a rather coarse and
invasive subject up to 80cm tall, with matt-green,
spear-shaped leaves and clusters of flesh-pink single
flowers. Europe, widely naturalized. Jul.-Sept. ☼☽
'Rosa Plena' - is more often grown, the flowers less
elegant and double, but rose pink. **Vaccaria** *S.
vaccaria (= Vaccaria pyramidata)* (**2**) HA is an erect
plant up to 75cm tall with lance-shaped leaves and
lax-branched clusters of rose or white flowers with
inflated, winged calyces. S. Europe - often as a weed.

3

Jul.-Aug. ☼ More showy than Annual Gypsophila, which it somewhat resembles. **Sweet William** *Dianthus barbatus* (**3**) HP or short-lived P, scarcely needs introduction, yet it is hardly as popular as it once was, perhaps due to gardeners' general dislike of biennial plants. It is a coarse plant with leafy dull-green clumps in the first year. In the second year, leafy stems rise 30-50cm high, bearing flat-topped masses of small fringed flowers in shades of pink, magenta, crimson, scarlet or white, the petals often banded or spotted and with a dark eye. Deliciously fragrant. An easy plant on most garden soils, though disliking acid ones. Europe. Jun.-Jul. ☼●△

DAISY FAMILY is by far the largest and most important family of garden flowers, with many species and cultivars, most of them with daisy- or thistle-like blossoms, often providing bold splashes of colour throughout the summer months. A great number of the most popular flowers belong here: Chrysanthemums, Dahlias, Marigolds, Michaelmas Daisies. Sunflowers and Zinnias. **Ageratum** *Ageratum houstonianum* (**1**) HHA is a charming little Mexican species, truly a perennial, though generally grown as an annual. It is one of those useful plants, like Alyssum and Lobelia, widely used for edging borders in more formal gardens. Plants form dense masses of heart-shaped leaves, 15-25cm tall, and throughout the summer they are smothered in fluffy balls of small powder-blue, rose or mauve flowers. The dwarfer strains are the finest. Jun.-Sept. ○ **Arctotis** *Arctotis aurea* (= *Venidium fastuosum*) (**2**) HHA, often called

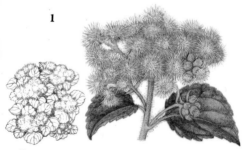

1

2

3

'Venidium Arctotis', is one of many gems from South Africa. Plants are rather straggly, reaching 45cm tall with ragged, lobed leaves. the large daisy flowerheads open widely in sunshine, vivid orange-yellow with a deep brownish-purple base to the rays surrounding the dark purple disk. Jul.-Aug. ☼△ *Ursinia versicolor* (**3**) is similar but more refined, bushier and seldom as tall, with smaller bright orange flowerheads with a deep violet, almost black, centre. S. Africa. ☼△

DAISY FAMILY (contd) **Michaelmas Daisies** are a popular group of late-flowering plants for the herbaceous border. Most are vigorous and adaptable plants which need dividing every two or three years, otherwise they become too congested and less floriferous. *Aster novi-belgii* (**2**) is the true Michaelmas Daisy with stout stems up to 1.5m tall, though often less, and broad masses of small daisy flowers, blue-violet in the species. N. America. Aug.-Oct. ☼△ Many cultivars from tall to dwarf ones are available. 'Jenny' (**3**) - red, semi-double, 50cm. *A. novae-angliae* (**1**) is similar but more vigorous, with flowerheads, each 2.5-3.5cm across, purple with a

yellow disk. Central N. America. Aug.-Oct. ☼△
Aster amellus (**4**) HP is a loose tufted plant, 45-60cm
tall, with crowded oblong leaves. The flowerheads,
3.5-6cm across, are in loose clusters, pale lavender to
reddish-purple. Plants often need some support. C. &
S. Europe. Jul.-Sept. ☼☻△ 'Frikartii' - lavender
blue. 90cm; 'King George' - rich violet-blue, 80cm;
'Moreheim Gem' - deep blue, 75cm; 'Violet Queen'
- 45cm. *A. sedifolius* (**5**) HP is another tufted perennial,
only 45-60cm tall. The rather ragged-looking flowerheads, each 1.8cm across, in flat-topped clusters, are
soft blue with a yellowish disk. C. & S. Europe, W.
Asia. Aug.-Sept. ☼☻

51

DAISY FAMILY (contd) **China Aster** *Callistephus chinensis* (**1**) HHA is one of the most widely grown border annuals and a fine cut flower, succeeding on most average garden soils. An erect branched plant up to 70cm tall. The large flowerheads are up to 12cm across, pink, red, crimson, purple, blue or white, with a yellowish disk. Nurserymen supply both single and double forms as well as the so-called 'Ostrich Plume Asters'. China. Jul.-Sept. ☼△ **Fleabanes** *Erigeron* are rather like refined Asters. Many of the modern cultivars are neater and more colourful than their ancestors. Most are derived from two North American species, *E. macranthus* and *E. speciosus*. The best of these are: 'Adria' - lavender blue, 75cm; 'Charity' (**2**) - pink, 60cm; 'Prosperity' - pale blue,

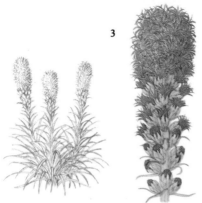

semi-double, 45cm; 'Rotes Meer' - red, semi-double, 50cm; 'Sincerity' - mauve. Quite different is the Mexican *E. mucronatus*, with small, white, lawn-daisy flowers turning pink. May-Oct. ☼△ **Blazing Star** *Liatris pycnostachys* (**3**) HP does not immediately look like a member of the daisy family. Plants form tufts of narrow grassy leaves from which arise bold stiff spikes, up to 1m tall, of dense fluffy purple and red flowers. The spikes are unusual in opening from the top downwards. S. USA. Jul.-Sept. ☼◐△ *L. spicata* is similar but less robust, rarely exceeding 70cm. 'Kobold' - very fine, only 60cm, with deep lilac-purple spikes. The Blazing Stars are superb border plants revelling in most ordinary garden soils. The spikes are being increasingly sold by florists.

1

DAISY FAMILY (contd) **Swan River Daisy** *Brachycome iberidifolia* (**1**) HHA is a charming daisy from West Australia, so it requires the sunniest site that can be found in the garden. It is an erect annual, 30cm tall, with numerous wiry stems and finely cut leaves. The solitary flowerheads occur in purple, pink, blue or white, usually with a darker centre. Under glass this will make a striking and rather dainty pot plant. Jul.-Sept. ☼ **Blanket Flower** *Gaillardia pulchella* (**2**) HAA is a hardy annual, up to 45cm tall, with lance-shaped or cut leaves and bold flat flowerheads, velvety brownish-red, the petals (rays) often tipped yellow, Most garden cultivars are hybrids with the perennial *G. aristata*, inheriting larger flowers and a perennial habit. N. America. Jun.-Sept. ☼☽△ 'Croftway Yellow' - shorter, clear yellow flowers; 'Mandarin' - to 90cm, flame-orange flowerheads. **Helenium** is a popular autumn flower, forming stiff tufts 60-150cm tall, with winged stems and dull-green pointed leaves. The flowerheads have a large central boss and occur in shades of yellow, bronze and red. Garden varieties, all of which dislike dry soils, are hybrids between *Helenium autumnale* and *H. nudiflorum*. Both E. USA. Jul.-Sept. ☼☽△ 'Bressingham Gold' - 90cm; 'Coppelia' - copper-orange, 90cm; 'Waldtraud' (**3**) - orange-brown, 120cm.'

2

3

DAISY FAMILY (contd) **Marigold** *Calendula officinalis*
(**1**) HA has always been popular in gardens and at one
time was grown as a pot herb, the flowerheads were
used to colour butter or as an addition to salads.
Garden forms are coarse, branched herbs, up to 80cm
tall, with pale, rough, rather wavy leaves and large
single or double flowerheads in shades of yellow and
orange. There are also forms with quilled petals. One
of the easiest of all annuals to grow. The wild form
comes from S. Europe and W. Asia. Jun.-Sept. ☼△
(For African and French Marigolds see pp. 81-2)
Christ's Eye *Inula oculus-Christi* (**2**) HP makes bold
clumps up to 50cm high. The pale yellow flowerheads
are solitary or loosely clustered. C. Europe and W.
Asia. Jul.-Aug. ☼☻ *I. orientalis* HP is finer with
broader leaves and orange-yellow, fine-rayed blooms.

2

3

I. royleana HP is altogether more striking, 1m tall or more, with oblong, heart-shaped leaves and large flowers, golden or orange with thread-like petals. Himalaya. Aug.-Oct. ☙ *Ligularia (= Senecio) clivorum* (**3**) HP is an imposing plant, 1m or more, with purplish stems and large heart-shaped leaves. The orange-yellow flowerheads occur in broad flat clusters. Moist soils. China and Japan. Jun.-Jul. ○☙ 'Desdemona' - purplish leaves. *L. stenocephala* HP, 150cm, has handsome rounded leaves. The slender spikes of golden flowers are borne on black stems. Asia. Jul.-Aug. ○☙ 'The Rocket' - a superb form.

DAISY FAMILY (contd) **Chrysanthemums** are a large and complex group containing many favourites. Most are easy to grow, the perennial types best when divided regularly. **Annual Chrysanthemum** *C. carinatum* (**1**) HA, 45cm tall, has finely divided leaves and large solitary flowerheads, of white, yellow, pink or crimson, but often with banded colours. A popular annual. N. Africa. Jul.-Aug. ☼△ **Pyrethrum** *C. coccineum* HP forms tufts 60cm tall with finely divided 'ferny' foliage. The solitary flowerheads are pink, red or white, with a yellow disk. Very free-flowering. W. Asia. May-Jul. ☼△ 'E.M.Robinson' (**2**)- pink; 'Kelway's Glorious' (**3**) - red; 'Queen Mary' - pink, double; 'Madeleine' - white, double. **Shasta Daisy** *Chrysanthemum maximum* HP, like a large Ox-eye Daisy, *C. leucanthemum* (**5**), is a robust plant to 1.2m with stiff stems and large flowerheads, pure white with a yellow 'eye'. S.W. Europe. Jul.-Sept. ☼☯△ 'Esther Read' (**6**) - 75cm, double white, the best; 'Wirral Supreme' - another fine double; 'H. Seibert' - 75cm. has frilled petals. **Feverfew** *C. parthenium* (**4**) HP is a popular herb for tea and for treating migraine. A stiff pungent plant, with dissected foliage and masses of small daisies. W. Asia. Jun.-Aug. ☼☯△ 'Aureum' - yellow-leaved form; 'Flore-pleno' - double flowers.

DAISY FAMILY (contd) **Chrysanthemum** *Chrysan-themum morifolium* is one of the most popular of all flowers, cultivated from ancient times in the Far East. Most cultivars are not hardy outside but there are some fine hardy sorts. The best are the spray varieties of *C. rubellum* (**1**), 60-80cm tall, with double and single flowers, mostly in pastel shades. Aug.-Oct. ☼ 'Clara Curtis' (**2**) - single, pink, very fine; 'Duchess of Edinburgh' - coppery-red; 'Pennine Gloss' - single yellow; 'Pennine Signal' - crimson; 'Peterkin' - light

5

6

orange, double. **Anthemis** *Anthemis tinctoria* (3) HP is like a tall Pyrethrum with bright yellow flowers. S. Europe. Jun.-Aug. ☼△ 'Crallach Gold'; 'Mrs E.C. Buxton' - primrose-yellow flowers. **Calliopsis** *Coreopsis grandiflora* (4) HP is a graceful, tufted plant with stiff stems bearing larger golden flowers, single or double. Very showy. E. USA. ☼△ 'Badengold'; 'Perry's Var.' *C. verticillata* (5) HP forms stiff tufts, up to 70cm tall, with fine ferny foliage and numerous small golden daisies. S.E. USA. Jul.-Sept. ☼☻ 'Grandiflora' - the best cultivar.

1

2

DAISY FAMILY (contd) **Cornflower** *Centaurea cyanus*
(**1**) HA was once a common flower in European
cornfields. It is an erect, rather ungainly plant, up to
1m tall. The typical small flowerheads occur in blue,
pink, purple or white. Dwarfer strains are available
which require little support. Europe. Jun.-Aug. ☼△
Sweet Sultan *C. moschata* (**2**) HA is a glorious plant
that deserves to be more widely planted. It grows
erect, 30-60cm tall, with cut green foliage and large
'cornflowers', yellow, rose-pink, purple or white.
Sweetly scented. Not as easy to succeed with as the
Cornflower, but well worth a try. W. Asia. Jul.-Aug.

☼△ *Centaurea dealbata* HP is a tufted, rather untidy plant with narrow, lobed leaves. The flowerheads are rose-purple and very handsome, borne on stems up to 50cm tall. W. Asia. May-Jul. ☼ 'John Coutts' (**3**) - lovely clear pink, the best form. **Hardheads** *C. montana* HP is common in gardens, forming invasive creeping tufts with stems up to 60cm tall. The flowerheads are violet-blue, like broad spidery cornflowers. Best in the wild garden. Europe. May-Jul. ☼◑ 'Alba' - white flowers; 'Violetta' (**4**) - the finest blue form.

DAISY FAMILY (contd) *Centaurea pulcherrima* (**1**) HP from the Caucasus and Asia Minor is a handsome, stiffly erect perennial, up to 90cm tall, with oblong, lobed leaves, grey-green above, whitish beneath. The large flowerheads are solitary, rosy-purple, but surrounded by numerous white papery bracts. **Yellow Knapweed** *C. macrocephala* (**2**) HP is a bold and imposing plant forming large tufts up to 130cm tall with coarse, rather ugly, oblong green leaves. The flowerheads are large, like yellow thistles, but soft.

The foliage should be guarded against caterpillars. W. Asia. Jul.-Aug. ☼★ **Cosmos** or **Cosmea** is an annual or perennial herb from Mexico with erect tough stems and opposite pairs of finely cut leaves. The relatively large daisy-flowers have broad overlapping petals. *C. bipinnatus* (**3**) HA is the most popular and a useful cut flower during the late summer. Plants, rather stiff and usually well-branched, grow up to 180cm in the most vigorous strains. Flowerheads white, rosy-pink, mauve, purple or reddish. Jul.-Sept. ☼△ *C. atrosanguineus* HHA has coarser leaves and distinctive dark crimson flowerheads. Jul.-Aug. ☼⬤

3

1

2

3

DAISY FAMILY (contd) **Dahlias** are amongst the most widely grown of all summer flowers in gardens. They are often grown competitively for showing. They combine many fine qualities, ease of growing, a prolonged flowering season and lack of diseases, as well as making excellent cut flowers. The wild ancestors of the *Dahlia* come from C. America. Today there are many types of Dahlias from short bedding types to tall ones, single- and double-flowered forms. The **Dwarf Bedding** types are extremely useful and generally grown from seed annually. They reach

4   5

30-50cm tall and bear single or semi-single flowers in all colours but blue. (**3**). The remaining groups are grown as HHP increased from cuttings or by division of the fleshy tubers. **Collarette** types, such as 'Fashion Monger' (**1**) and 'Alstergrass' (**2**) are also single-flowered but the 'eye' (disk) of the flowerhead has a number of short uneven petals, often white, around the edge. They are unusual but of little use as a cut flower. The **Pompom** types (**4**) have small rounded, fully double, flowers and grow up to 90cm tall. The **Anemone-flowered**, such as 'Comet' (**5**) are single-flowered but with a pin-cushion mass of short petals in the centre of the flowerhead.

DAISY FAMILY **Dahlias** (contd) The **Decorative**
group, most popular of all, have fully double
flowerheads with numerous broad petals, as in 'Duet'
(**1**) and 'Gerrie Hack' (**2**). They are usually divided by
the specialist into small, medium and giant sizes.
Cactus Dahlias are similar but the petals are rolled
back along their margins, giving a quilled, pointed
appearance. Again there are small-, medium- and
large-flowered forms. Among many hundreds of
cultivars are 'Nantenan' (**3**) and 'Drakenburg' (**4**).

3

4

Except in the mildest areas, Dahlia tubers should be lifted once the foliage has been frosted in the autumn, the stems trimmed back and the tubers dried before storing them in a frost-free place. Inspect them regularly for signs of rot and treat them accordingly. Tubers can be brought into growth in the early spring by placing them in shallow boxes of soil or peat. Cuttings of vigorous young shoots, 10-14cm long, root readily in a warm place and are the easiest means of increasing stock. Jul.-Sept. ☼☀☁△

DAISY FAMILY (contd) **Dimorphotheca** *Dimorphotheca sinuata* (= *D. aurantiaca*) (**1**) HHA is an attractive, spreading herb 30cm tall with bright orange or yellow daisy flowers borne on slender stalks, each flowerhead with a violet disk. Needs a dry sunny place to be seen at its best. S. Africa. Jul.-Sept. ☼ *D. pluvialis* is similar but the flowerheads are glistening white, violet-blue in the centre. The related *Osteospermum barberiae* (**2**) HHP is practically hardy in the mildest districts, a tufted subshrub up to 45cm tall

3

4

with large rosy-purple or white flowerheads opening
in sunshine. Easily grown and floriferous. S. Africa.
Jun.-Sept. ☼ 'Molly Gould' - rose-crimson flowers.
Echinacea *Echinacea purpurea* (= *Rudbeckia purpurea*) HP is a handsome erect tufted plant, 60-90cm
tall. The large flowerheads are rosy-purple, the broad
ray petals swept downwards around a boss-like disk.
C. USA. Jul.-Sept. ☼△ 'Robert Bloom' (**3**) - blooms
over a long season on 90cm stems; 'White Lustre' (**4**) -
the finest white selection.

DAISY FAMILY (contd) **Everlasting Flower** *Helichrysum bracteatum* (**1**) HHA is one of the most popular of all flowers for drying. Plants are erect and coarse-looking, up to 80cm tall, with dull green leaves of little appeal. The characteristic papery flowerheads are globular at first, yellow, brown, maroon, purplish or white, gradually opening to reveal a yellowish flat disk and much loved by butterflies. Good on most ordinary soils, best raised under glass initially. For drying, the flowerheads should be cut as they open and hung in bunches upside down. E. & S.E. Australia. Jul.-Oct. ☼★△ **Pearly Everlasting** *Anaphalis margaritacea* (**2**) HP is a tufted grey-green

1

2

3

plant up to 50cm tall, with lance-shaped leaves and dense flattish clusters of small, milky white, papery flowerheads. E. North America. Jul.-Sept. ☼★△
Treasure Flower *Gazania ringens (= G. splendens)* (**3**) HHP is a spectacular plant for warm sheltered places, often used for bedding schemes, especially in coastal regions. Plants form loosely tangled clumps, up to 30cm tall, with brittle stems and rather leathery, narrow, often lobed, green or white-felted leaves. The large flowerheads are solitary, opening widely in strong sunshine, cream, yellow, golden-orange, purple or bronze, the petals often blotched or banded near the base. The best coloured forms should be increased from cuttings which root readily in late summer and these should be overwintered under glass. S. Africa. Jun.-Sept. ☼

1

DAISY FAMILY (contd) **Globe Artichoke** *Cynara scolymus* (**1**) HP is a handsome plant for the back of the border. The large acanthus-like leaves form bold tufts and, in mid-summer, the stout stems rise up to 180cm tall, carrying huge 'thistle heads' with vivid violet-blue shaving brush middles. They are eaten in bud and superb for drying. Origin uncertain. Jul.-Sept. ☼★△ **Cardoon** *C. cardunculus* is equally satisfactory, often mistaken for the previous, but even more

2

vigorous with rather smaller, more spiny, flowerheads. S. Europe. Aug.-Sept. ☼★△ **Globe Thistle**
Echinops ritro (**2**) HP is an erect thistle-like plant with
stiff stems up to 1m tall, with spiky, deeply cut leaves,
green above but whitish beneath. The solitary
spherical flowerheads are a fine metallic blue. Much
loved by bees. Good on most soils. S. Europe.
Jul.-Sept. ☼★ *E. sphaerocephalus* is taller with
broader, thankfully less prickly, leaves and larger
flowerheads. Commonly grown. 'Taplow Blue' -
120m tall, magnificent, with flowerheads brighter
blue than most.

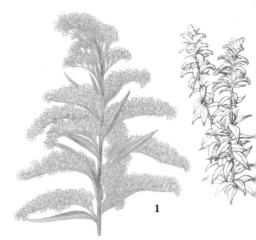

1

DAISY FAMILY (contd) **Golden Rod** *Solidago* HP are well-known, widely-grown North American perennials. The cultivated varieties have a complex origin involving *S. canadensis*, *S. gigantea* and *S. rugosa*. All are tufted perennials with stiff leafy stems and broad one-sided panicles of numerous small yellow flowers. Many of the best cultivars have a more compact habit and finer coloured flowers. They are amongst the easiest plants to grow, revelling in well-drained soils. Aug.-Oct. ☼△ 'Goldenmosa' (**1**) - 75cm, golden yellow, one of the best; 'Golden Shower' - 75cm, bright yellow; 'Lerraft' - 75cm, golden; 'Lemore' - similar but lemon-yellow; 'Mimosa' - 150cm, deep yellow. **Hawkweeds** are mostly far too invasive for the average garden, however, there are two worthy of a corner somewhere. **Fox and Cubs** *Hieracium aurantiacum* (**2**) HP is a creeping plant with oblong leaves and delicate stems, 30cm tall, carrying several small brick-red 'dandelion' flowerheads. C. Europe. Jun.-Jul. ☼☻ *H. brunneo-croceum* is even more rampant, with narrower leaves and paler brownish-orange flowerheads. **Tidy Tips** *Layia elegans* (**3**) HHA is a small Californian annual, up to 25cm tall, with narrow strap leaves and solitary small, yellow flowerheads with white-tipped petals. Charming, though not spectacular by any means. California. Jul.-Aug. ☼

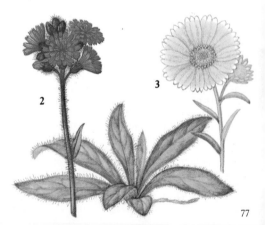

DAISY FAMILY (contd) **Leopard's Bane** *Doronicum* are cheerful bright yellow daisies for the spring garden. *D. orientale* (= *D. caucasicum*) (**1**) HP is a tufted plant up to 45cm tall with heart-shaped leaves and large, 5-7cm diameter, flowerheads. W. Asia. Mar.-Apr. ☼☽△ *D. pardalianches* (**2**) is altogether more robust, up to 90cm tall, with clusters of smaller flowerheads. C. & S. Europe. May-Jun. All are easily grown but the best are the named cultivars. 'Goldzwerg' - 15cm; 'Harpur Crewe' - 90cm, an old

3

favourite; 'Miss Mason' - 50cm; 'Spring Beauty' -
40cm, large double flowers. **Marigolds** *Tagetes* Both
the popular African and French Marigolds come
under this heading. All are strongly aromatic, rather
gaudy plants, widely used for mass bedding schemes.
African Marigold *T. erecta* (**3**) HHA is a robust stiff
plant, 60-120cm tall, with deeply cut leaves and large,
rather formless, foamy flowerheads in shades of
yellow or orange. Most strains have overbloated
blooms, though admittedly impressive. The singles
would be far finer if available. Mexico (despite their
common name). Jul.-Sept. ☼

DAISY FAMILY (contd) **French Marigold** *Tagetes patula* HHA is a more refined plant, seldom exceeding 30cm tall, often smaller, forming a neat bushy plant with deeply dissected, deep green leaves. The small flowerheads are single or double in cultivated strains, varying in colour from yellow to orange to velvety dark crimson-brown, or yellow flecked with orange-brown or crimson. Mexico. Jul.-Sept. 'Tiger Eyes' (**1**); 'Teeny Weeny' (**2**); 'Holiday Crested' (**3**); 'Queen Beatrix' (**4**). *For Marigold (Calendula) see p. 58* **Red Sunflower** *Tithonia rotundifolia (= T. speciosa)* HHA is one of those spectacular plants that is suprisingly little seen in gardens, but well deserves a place there, for it is a good gap filler at the back of the herbaceous border. The plants are stout and erect, 120-190cm tall or more, with a habit not unlike the well-known Annual Sunflower. The coarse hairy leaves are broad, almost heart-shaped and often lobed. The flower-heads are smaller than the sunflower, only one third the size, but with an eye-catching orange and scarlet coloration. Seeds are best sown under glass and young plants placed out-of-doors at the end of May. C. America. Jul.-Sept. ☼ 'Torch' (5) - a splendid large-flowered form, even more richly coloured.

5

1

2

DAISY FAMILY (contd) **Rudbeckias** are a group of
handsome, coarsely hairy, plants. All require plenty
of sun and moisture. **Black-eyed Susan** *E. speciosa*
(= *R. newmannii*) (**1**) HP is the finest, tufted to 60cm
tall with oval leaves and rich golden yellow flowers
with a purplish-black central boss. C. USA. July-
Sept. ○△ 'Goldstrum' - very fine form, 90cm;
'Goldquelle' - double chrome-yellow flowers, 90cm.
R. bicolor (**2**) HA grows to 45cm tall with large flowers,

3

either all yellow or crimson, or yellow with a bronzed centre. There are also double forms. Texas. Jul.-Sept.

☼△ **Stokesia** *Stokesia laevis* (**3**) HP is a curious though attractive plant, only rarely seen in gardens. It is not unlike a large short Cornflower, forming spreading tufts 30-45cm tall, with rather pale green, narrow leaves tapering to the winged stalk. The large flowers, 5cm across, are blue, but fade as they age. A plant for a good well-drained loam. The individual flowers are not long-lived but are produced in profusion on established plants. S.E. & C. USA. Jul.-Sept. ☼ 'Blue Moon'- the finest cultivar, more richly coloured than some forms.

1

DAISY FAMILY (contd) **Annual Sunflower** *Helianthus annus* HHA Few flowers are better known than this stout annual herb, grown primarily for the fascination of its huge flowers. Despite the fact that there are annual competitions to produce the tallest specimen, the sunflower has declined as a garden plant in recent years. The characteristic fruit heads are loved by finches and tits. W. USA. Aug.-Oct. ☼★ **Perennial Sunflower** *H. decapetalus* (**1**) HP is a better garden plant, 1m tall or more. The branched flower stems bear several golden yellow flowerheads. An easily grown plant. There are also double-flowered forms.

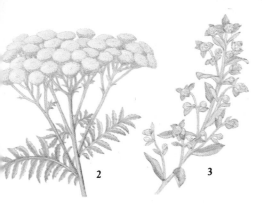

N. America. Aug.-Oct. ☼△ 'Loddon Gold' - fully double flowers; 'Morning Sun' - rich yellow, anemone-centred, flowers. **Tansy** *Tanacetum vulgare* (**2**) HP is a strongly aromatic plant with stiff erect stems to 80cm tall, bearing small globular yellow flowerheads. Easy on most soil types. Europe. Aug.-Sept. ☼△ **Artemisias** are aromatic perennials with insignificant flowers but attractive foliage. *A. lactiflora* grows to 120cm tall, with dull, rather ragged, green leaves and sprays of creamy-white flowers. A rather weedy plant. China. Aug.-Oct. ☼☻ *A. pontica* HP is finer, up to 60cm tall, with erect stems and a silver filigree of finely divided leaves. C. & E. Europe and W. Asia. Jul.-Aug. ☼ There are several good named cultivars: 'Lambrook Silver' (**3**) - 90cm; 'Powys Castle' - 60cm; 'Silver Queen' - 75cm.

DAISY FAMILY (contd) **Vernonia** *Vernonia nove-boracensis* (**1**) HP is a stout erect tufted plant for the back of a border, reaching up to 180cm tall, with purplish stems and numerous lance-shaped, deep green leaves which have a serrated margin. The small thistle-like flowerheads are borne in wide, rounded, purple masses at the tops of the stems. Sometimes found in catalogues as *V. arkansana*. E. USA. Aug.-Sept. ☼☽ *V. crinita* is taller, up to 220cm high, with crimson-purple flowers. S. USA. Sept.-Nov. **Yarrows** and **Milfoils** *Achillea* are a very large group

1

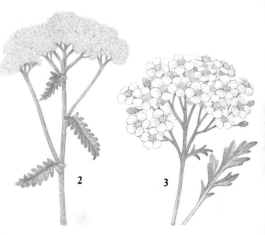

of mostly rather pungent perennials with characteristic small flowers borne in large flat clusters. They generally thrive in sunny places in well-drained soils. The yellow ones are particularly good for drying. *A. clavennae* (**3**) HP grows only 20cm tall with oblong silvery-grey, somewhat cut leaves. The relatively large flowerheads are white. C. & S. Europe. Jun.-Aug. ☼ The fine hybrid between this and *A. tomentosa* (**2**), with its taller stems, silvery-grey foliage and sulphur- or cream-coloured flowers is often sold under the name 'King Henry'. 'Moonshine' is even finer with its silvery foliage and pale yellow flowerheads on stems up to 60cm tall. Jun.-Aug. ☼ △

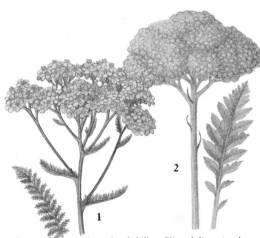

DAISY FAMILY (contd) *Achillea filipendulina* (= *A. eupatorium*) HP from Asia Minor, forms erect tufts up to 120cm tall. The large compact flower heads are bright golden yellow and very handsome. Jul.-Sept. ☼★△ *A. millefolium* HP, a native European species, is vigorous though not too invasive. Good colour forms have been selected over the years: 'Cerise Queen' (**1**) - 75cm, crimson flowers; 'Gold Plate' (**2**) - the finest, up to 150cm tall, with large flowerheads. **Sneezewort** *A. ptarmica*, also European, is neater with tufts up to 75cm tall, excellent for borders. Jun.-Aug. ☼◐△ 'Perry's White' and 'The Pearl' - both excellent double white varieties.

Zinnias *Z.elegans* HHA is a great favourite amongst gardeners but not always easy to please. It requires sunny warm sheltered areas and good rich soils, and does particularly well during long hot summers, the large flowers and exotic appearance attracting much attention. The plant grows to 30-90cm tall with broad, rough, paired leaves and erect stems. The solitary large flowerheads, borne on thickened stalks, come in a wide variety of colours: scarlet, orange, yellow, pink, purple, mauve and white. Many forms are offered by seedsmen, both single- (**3**) and double-flowered (**4**). Mexico. Jul.-Sept. ☼ △

TRADESCANTIA FAMILY An extensive, primarily tropical, family with short-lived flowers, but produced in abundance. **Virginia Spiderwort** *Tradescantia virginiana* (**1**) HP forms grassy tufts up to 45cm tall, with bright clusters of large three-petalled flowers, white, blue or purple. E. USA. Jun.-Sept. ☼☽ There are some fine cultivars, all easy accommodating plants, readily increased by division of the clumps after they cease to flower: 'Carmine Glow' - neater habit than most; 'Isis' - deep blue; 'Osprey' - white; 'Purewell Giant' - carmine purple; 'Zwaneburg Blue' - blue flowers, exceptionally large.

1

2

STONECROP FAMILY is an extensive family of succulent plants with small, often star-shaped, flowers. **Ice Plant** *Sedum spectabilie* (**2**) HP is an easy and extremely popular plant for a sunny position in most types of soil. Plants form thick mounded tufts up to 45cm tall with broad rounded thick, grey-green, smooth leaves. The flowers are crammed closely together into characteristic flattened heads, rose-pink or red. The great glory of this plant is its attraction to butterflies in the late summer. China and Japan. Aug.-Oct. ☼ 'Autumn Joy' - 60cm, salmon-pink flowers, is the finest form; 'Brilliant' - deep pink flowers, only 35cm; 'Variegatum' - yellow leaf variations, pink flowers.

1

2

MORNING GLORY FAMILY Beside the Bindweeds, often troublesome weeds in gardens, this family contains some fine garden plants. *Convolvulus elegantissima* (**1**) HP is an untidy sprawling plant with grey foliage, some leaves heart-shaped, others deeply-lobed. The pink flowers are its best feature. S. Europe. Jul.-Sept. ☼ *C. tricolor* (**2**) HA is the easiest to grow, up to 45cm tall, laxly branched with eye-catching, almost startling flowers. S. Europe. Jul.-Sept. ☼ **Morning Glory** *Ipomoea tricolor (= I. rubrocaerulea)* (**3**) HHA One of the most spectacular

3

4

plants but susceptible to low temperatures and
resenting disturbance. Plants twine up to 2m or more.
The large salver-shaped flowers are short-lived but
exquisite, one of the finest of all blues in our gardens.
C. America. Jul.-Sept. ☼☽ 'Heavenly Blue' -
unsurpassed in beauty. *I. purpurea* (**4**) HHA is more
vigorous, with dark green heart-shaped leaves,
sometimes lobed, and clusters of smaller flowers,
purple, crimson or occasionally white. Both this and
I. tricolor require a warm sheltered corner of the
garden and a fence, pea sticks or trellis to climb up.
C. America. Jul.-Sept. ☼

WALLFLOWER FAMILY is a large temperate family containing some popular garden flowers. **Yellow Alyssum** *Alyssum saxatile* (**1**) HP is a low hummock-forming plant with dense tufts of grey elliptical leaves and effective sprays of tiny golden flowers. Good along path edges. S. Europe. Apr.-Jun. ☼ 'Citrinum' - pale yellow flowers. **White Alyssum** *Lobularia maritima* (**2**)HA is widely grown, quick to flower from seed and often interplanted with Lobelia along the edge of borders. It is a low spreading plant with narrow grey leaves and terminal heads of small white, honey-scented flowers. Mediterranean. Jun.-Oct. ☼ 'Snow Cloth' and 'Little Dorrit' - both compact forms, pure white flowers. Coloured forms include: 'Violet Queen'. Pink Heather'. 'Royal Carpet' - purple flowers.

2

1

Arabis, often known as Rock Cress, is a popular garden flower, ideal for the edge of borders on paths. The common one is *A. caucasica* (**3**) HP, forming a low creeping mat of soft greyish leaves and covered in clusters of pure white flowers in the spring, rising to 15cm tall. E. Mediterranean. Apr.-Jun. ☼ 'Plena' - double white flowers. Hybrids with another species, *A. aubretioides*, have produced some fine rose-pink cultivars. The best of these is 'Rosa Bella'. *A. blepharophylla* from California is less rampant with striking carmine-pink flowers, but scarcely as hardy as the previous species. ☼ **Aubretia** *Aubretia deltoidea* (**4**) HP forms leafy cushions, 7-10cm high, smothered in mauve or purple flowers in spring. S. Europe. Apr.-Jun.

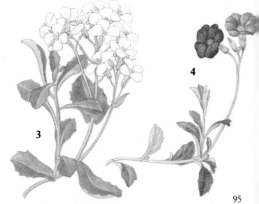

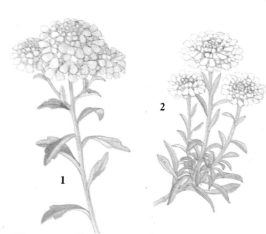

WALLFLOWER FAMILY (contd) **Candytufts** are easily recognized by their lopsided flowers, each with two long and two short petals. **Perennial Candytuft** *Iberis sempervirens* (**2**) HP forms a low spreading evergreen, rather flat bush, 30cm tall, with and heads of small white flowers. Apr.-Jun. ☼ 'Snowflake' - the finest form. **Annual Candytuft** *I. amara* (**1**) and *I. umbellata* HA are both commonly grown. The former is more slender, with narrow, lobed leaves and white or lilac flowers. The latter has bolder clusters of lilac, pink or magenta flowers. Both are European in origin and easy to grow, though not remaining in bloom for very long. Jul.-Aug. ☼

Honesty *Lunaria annua* (**3**) HB is another popular cottage garden flower grown as much for its flowers as for the striking fruits. It is one of the easiest plants to grow, spreading around freely in in most soils. In the first year plants make a lax rosette of coarse, heart-shaped leaves. During the second year the stem rises up to 1m carrying a wide branching head of colourful purple or white flowers which are fragrant and much liked by early butterflies. In the autumn the fruit discs split to leave a silvery membrane (**4**) so characteristic of the plant. Best on rather poor soils, doing well in difficult corners of the garden, particularly beneath hedges. S.E. Europe and the Middle East. Apr.-May. ☼◐★ 'Variegata' - less likeable form with blotched leaves and striped flowers, more a curiosity than of any real merit.

3

4

WALLFLOWER FAMILY (contd) **Wallflower** *Cheiranthus cheiri* (**1**) HB is a widely used bedding plant as popular today as ever. Although strictly speaking a perennial, plants are treated as biennial and are generally discarded after flowering to make way for summer bedding plants. The racemes of flowers are wonderfully scented and come in a range of velvety colours. As cut flowers they should have their water changed daily. Europe. Mar.-May. ☼△ *Erysimum linifolium* HHP has the habit and look of a Wallflower. Plants form dense bushes up to 50cm. The slender flower-spikes bear lilac-purple, bronzing flowers.

Spain and Portugal. Apr.-Aug. ☼ 'E.A. Bowles' (**2**)
- the finest form, easy from cuttings. **Siberian
Wallflower** *E. perofskianum* (**3**) HB is another fine
bedding plant, up to 60cm high, bearing fragrant
brilliant orange flowers, loved by butterflies. There is
a yellow variety. Asia. Apr.-Jul. ☼△ Some fine
hybrids exist between these and the true Wallflower:
'Constant Cheer' - violet-mauve with a hint of bronze;
'Jacob's Ladder'- flowers orange, changing to bronze
and lilac; 'Orange Flame'.

WALLFLOWER FAMILY (contd) **Stocks** There are various plants which come under this heading. **Virginia Stock** *Malcolmia maritima* (**1**) HA is a bright, rather slight plant, up to 20cm tall, with narrow greyish leaves and small gay racemes of pink, purple, greenish-yellow or white flowers. Mediterranean. May-Oct., with repeated sowings. ☼ **Night-scented Stock** *Matthiola bicornis* (**2**) HA is a sprawling herb with slender racemes of small, sweetly-scented, pinkish-purple flowers, opening in the evening. S.E. Europe & Asia Minor. Jun.-Sept. ☼☽ **Garden Stock** *Matthiola incana* (**4**) HHP forms a coarse

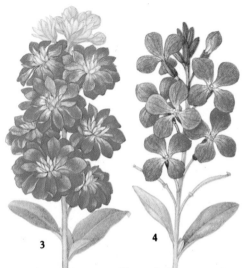

3   **4**

grey-leaved plant up to 75cm tall. Flowers are large and borne in dense racemes, wonderfully clove-scented, in a range of colours, though pink and purple predominate. Quick-maturing, double-flowered, forms are widely grown, as are the slower, over-wintering 'Brompton Stocks' (var. *hiberna*)(**3**). All like a rich soil, preferably alkaline, and are best raised under glass. Larger seedlings in the same batch are generally single, richly fragrant forms. Mediterranean. May-Sept. ☼△

WALLFLOWER FAMILY (contd) **Sweet Rocket** or
Dame's Violet *Hesperis matronalis* (**1**) HP is a
favourite old cottage garden flower, often scorned in
modern gardens, but particularly fine naturalised on
grassy banks or along hedgerows. A rather coarse
leafy, erect plant, up to 1m tall, with branched
panicles of fine white, pink or purple flowers,
fragrant and very attractive to butterflies. Can be
grown as a biennial. It is well worthwhile selecting the
better forms and propagating these frequently, by
division. Europe and W. Asia. Apr.-Jun. ☼☽

SCABIOUS FAMILY This primarily temperate family is characterised by the Scabious and Sheepsbit, *Succisa*, with rather daisy-like flowerheads, but it also contains thistle-like plants with spiny stems and leaves. The **Teasel** *Dipsacus fullonum* is very well-known, though not a particularly good garden plant. Jul.-Sept. **Morina** *Morina longifolia* (**2**) HP is an aristocratic plant with dense rosettes of shiny, narrow, spiny leaves. The rigid flower stems rise up to 70cm tall, bearing opposite pairs of spiny leaves below whorls of long-tubed flowers. The flowers open white but gradually turn to pink, then crimson. Good on most garden soils. Himalaya. Jun.-Sept. ☼❦

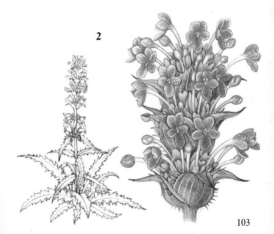

2

SCABIOUS FAMILY (contd) **Annual Scabious** *Scabious atropurpurea* (**1**) HA is a slender erect plant, 30-90cm tall, with dissected stem leaves. The pin-cushion flowers are borne on long stalks in a wide variety of colours from rich velvety-purple to crimson-lilac, mauve, pink or white. Mediterranean. Jul.-Sept.☼△ **Caucasian Scabious** *S. caucasica* (**2**) HP, deservedly popular, has large, rather flat flowerheads blue with a hint of lilac or mauve, on 75cm stems. There are also white or crimson forms. Caucasus & N. Iran. Jun.-Sept. ☼☻△ 'Bressingham White'; 'Clive Greaves' - a fine blue, the best of all.

SPURGE FAMILY These handsome plants, with a long flowering season, have small flowers surrounded by striking bracts, often green or red in colour. Broken stems and leaves exude a milky sap. **Caper Spurge** *Euphorbia lathyrus* HA is often seen in cottage gardens and can be a troublesome weed. The fruits are poisonous. Europe. Jul.-Sept. *E. polychroma* (**3**) HP is a very fine species, forming neat rounded hummocks 45cm high, with oblong leaves and tight flowerheads in a striking sulphur-yellow. It deserves a place in every garden. C. Europe. Apr.-Jun. ☼☽ *E. griffithii* is a most exciting plant when grown well, 30-70cm tall with slender leaves and dense clusters of glowing orange-red flowers. Himalaya. Apr.-May. ☼☽ 'Fireglow' (**4**) - the best form.

105

SPURGE FAMILY (contd) *Euphorbia characias* (**1**) HHP is a most imposing plant and guaranteed to attract attention. Plants form large tufts up to 1m high. A fine plant, surviving most average winters in warmer districts but not reliably hardy during severe weather. Established plants often seed around. Subsp. *wulfenii* is the finest form with broad apple-green flowerheads. S. Europe. May-July. ☼ *E. myrsinites* (**2**) HHP has sprawling stems, useful at the front of the border or path edge. S. Europe. May-Jul.

GENTIAN FAMILY is noted for the brilliance of its flowers. The species range from large leafy perennials to the daintiest and exquisite tufts from high mountain meadows. *Gentiana acaulis* (**3**) HP forms low tufts up to 10cm tall, bearing brilliant blue trumpet flowers in the spring. Plants require a sunny position but do not always flower well. An ideal rock garden plant. In the wild a plant of high alpine meadows; one of the most splendid European Alpines. C. Europe. May-June. ☼ *G. septemfida* (**4**) is dwarfer and more tufted, up to 25cm tall, with oblong, rather fleshy leaves and clusters of deep blue, green-spotted trumpets. Various forms can be purchased. W. Asia. July-September. ☙

3

4

GENTIAN FAMILY (contd) **Willow Gentian** *Gentiana asclepiadea* (**1**) HP is one of the easiest to grow, 60cm tall, its paired trumpet flowers borne only on the upper part of arching slender stems. There are pale blue and white forms. A plant for moist sites. C. Europe & E. Asia. Aug.-Sept. ☼● *Gentiana sino-ornata* (**2**) HP If one had to choose one species for the garden then this must surely be it. The plants form sprawling tufts. the large trumpet flowers are an exquisite deep kingfisher-blue and open in sunshine. Plants are best increased by dividing the thong-like roots. W. China. Sept.-Oct. ☼☽

GERANIUM FAMILY The **Geraniums** or **Cranesbills**
HP are amongst the most useful of all border flowers.
Geranium ibericum forms tufts up to 60cm tall. Its
large, clustered, flowers are vivid violet-blue, with
notched ends. W. Asia. June-July. ☼☾ Var.
platypetalum (**4**) is similar but the petals unnotched.
G. macrorrhizum is a pungent creeping plant, 30cm
tall, with reddish-purple flowers. C. & S. Europe.
May-July. ☼☾ 'Ingwersen's Variety' (**5**) - the finest.
G. endressii (**3**)forms large tufts up to 50cm tall with
satiny, salmon-pink flowers. S. Europe. Jun.-Sept.
☼☾ 'A.T.Johnson' - the best.

GERANIUM FAMILY (contd) *Geranium psilostemon* (= *G. armenum*) (**1**) HP is perhaps the most riveting of the hardy species, forming large loose tufts, up to 75cm tall. The flowers are a dazzling satiny magenta with an almost black centre, a rather strident colour but superb when carefully placed. W. Asia. May-Jul. ☼◐ **Meadow Cranesbill** *G. pratense* HP is a prolific grower, 60cm tall, bearing delicate blue-cupped flowers of great charm. Excellent in mixed borders or wild gardens. Europe & W. Asia. Jun.-Jul. ☼◐ 'Album Plenum'; 'Coeruleum Plenum' - double pale

blue; 'Kashmir White' (**2**); 'Mrs Kendall Clarke' - fine blue form; 'Johnson's Blue' (**3**) - clear bright blue, quite exquisite, of hybrid origin. **Bloody Cranesbill** *G. sanguineum* (**4**) HP forms a low spreading cushion plant, bearing solitary, saucer-shaped, magenta blooms over a long season. W. Europe. Jun.-Aug. ☼ 'Album' - fine white form; var. *lancastriense* - delightful pale pink flowers. **Dusky Cranesbill** *G. phaeum* (**5**) forms large, leafy tufts, 60cm tall, carrying numerous small dusky-purple flowers with the petals swept half back. Europe. June-July. ☼●

111

PHACELIA FAMILY comes primarily from North America. Two annual species are commonly grown in gardens. Both are easy on light well-drained soils. **Baby Blue Eyes** *Nemophila menziesii* (**1**) HA is a weak-stemmed herb, only 15cm tall, with lobed leaves. The delightful bowl-shaped flowers are a clear bright blue and borne in profusion. California. Jul.-Aug. ☼ *Phacelia campanularia* (**2**) HA, also from California, is even more appealing, up to 60cm tall, with heart-shaped leaves. The curved cymes bear a series of intense gentian-blue flowers. One of the best blue flowers in the annual border. Jun.-Sept. ☼

3

4

IRIS FAMILY contains many decorative species with grassy or sword-shaped leaves. **Kaffir Lily** *Schizostylis coccinea* (**3**) HHP has stems up to 70cm tall, bearing symmetrical flowers in a one-sided spike, red or pink. South Africa. Oct.-Nov.. ☼△ **Crocosmia** (including **Montbretias**) have curved red or orange flowers on branched spikes 60-100cm high. S. Africa. Jul.-Sept. ☼△ *C. masonorum* - 60cm with glowing orange sprays; 'Lucifer' - 100cm, flame red; 'Vulcan' - 75cm, orange-red; 'Emily Mackenzie' (**4**) - 60cm, orange with a crimson-brown throat.

IRIS FAMILY (contd) **Irises** are on the whole accommodating plants for a variety of situations, depending upon the type. Few flowers make more impression in borders. Both bulbous and rhizomatous species are grown. There are far too many to include them all here. **Stinking Iris** *Iris foetidissima* (**1**) HP is a European species, forming tough evergreen tufts up to 50cm tall. The flowers are rather small, dull purple or yellowish and neatly veined. They are followed in autumn by striking fruit capsules which split to reveal rows of scarlet seeds (**2**). Jun.-Jul. ☼●△ **Siberian Iris** *I. sibirica* (**3**) HP is one of the

114

4

most popular irises, forming dense grassy tufts, 90cm tall, with small bright blue flowers in profusion. Best on moist soils. June-July. ☼☽△ **German** or **Bearded Iris** *Iris germanica* is the well-known and widespread blue-purple flag Iris of gardens. Its stout rhizomes thrive in many soils but prefer well-drained sunny positions. The modern Bearded Irises (**4**) are of complex origin, involving various species, including *I. germanica*, *I. pallida* and *I. variegata* - all European in origin. This has given rise to an amazing range of colours, varying in height from 30cm to 150cm, with stiff, sword-shaped leaves. Catalogues often list dozens of varieties. May-Jun. ☼

1

2

IRIS FAMILY (contd) *Iris kaempferi* (**1**) HP is commonly cultivated in or near water. There are many named varieties in bold blues, purple, pink or white. Japan. Jun.-Jul. **Algerian Iris** *I. unguicularis* (= *I. stylosa*) HP flowers in the depths of winter. Few plants can be more welcome. The plants form dense coarse leafy tufts, 30cm tall, with large lavender blue, primrose-scented flowers. They need a sunny, warm, well-

3

4

drained site - one below a wall is perfect. S. & E.
Mediterranean. Dec.-Mar. ☼△ 'Mrs Barnard' (**2**) -
rich deep lavender-blue, the finest. **Bulbous Irises**
are popular florist flowers, good in open borders in
well-drained sunny positions. **English Iris** *I. latifolia*
(= *I. xiphioides*) (**3**) has large deep royal blue flowers
on 70cm stems. Jun.-Jul. Pyrenees. **Spanish Iris** *I.
xiphium* (**4**), also from S.W. Europe, is similar but
with more refined flowers in shades of blue or yellow.
Spain. Jun.-Aug. ☼◑△ 'Wedgewood' - the best
known.

IRIS FAMILY (contd) *Sisyrinchium striatum* (**1**) HP has flattened upright fans of sword-shaped leaves and slender 40-70cm spikes of small starry flowers. Individual flowers are short-lived but are produced in profusion. Chile. Jun.-Jul. ☼☼ *Libertia chilensis (= L. formosa)* (**2**) HHP is a robust and tufted plant with slender grassy leaves. Stiff flowering stems, 89cm tall, bear clusters of smallflowers. Prefers well-drained soils, often seeding itself freely once established. Chile. May-Jul. ☼

MINT FAMILY is a large family of temperate and tropical regions, containing many culinary and aromatic herbs: the Lavenders, Marjorams, Mints and Thymes are good examples. **Bells of Ireland** *Molucella laevis* (**3**) HHA is a much-branched plant, 75cm tall, with a rather gawky appearance. The flowers are borne in whorls, each with a conspicuous large, funnel-shaped, persistent green calyx, but with insignificant whitish corollas inside. Best raised under glass. An intriguing plant, excellent for drying when in full flower. Middle East. Jul.-Aug. ☼△

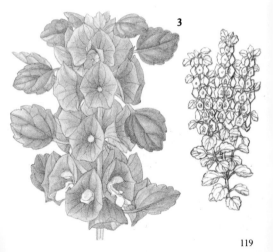

3

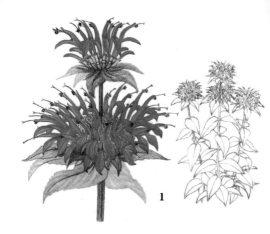

MINT FAMILY (contd) **Bergamot** *Monarda didyma* HP is a spreading plant with erect square stems, up to 90cm tall, and oval leaves, aromatic when crushed. The flowers are borne in characteristic dense whorls, purplish-red, scarlet or pink. A popular garden flower, requiring a moist, though well-drained, soil. Various American Indian tribes made Oswega Tea from an infusion of the leaves, which smell rather like Thyme. E. North America. Jul.-Sept. ☼☙△ Some fine cultivars are available, all easily grown: 'Cambridge Scarlet' (**1**) - an old favourite; 'Pillar Box'; 'Croftway Pink'; 'Prairie Night' - violet-purple; 'Snow Maiden'.

2

Bugle *Ajuga genevensis* (often mistaken for *A. pyramidalis* in catalogues) HP is a mat-forming plant with erect flowering stems up to 12cm tall. The spoon-shaped leaves form loose flattish rosettes and begin to wither as the plants come into flower. The spires of small vivid-blue flowers are surrounded by broad purplish, leaf-like bracts. A useful plant for average soils, fine for edging or exposed banks. Europe. May-Jun. ☼ 'Burgundy Glow' - leaves in several shades of wine-red, an eye-catcher; 'Multicolor' - leaves with pink, white, red or green mottling, quite startling; 'Purpurea' (**2**) - leaves reddish-purple; 'Variegata' - leaves buff and pale green.

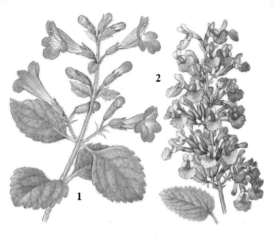

MINT FAMILY (contd) **Calamint** *Calamintha grandi-flora* (**1**)HA is a pretty, aromatic plant with rather sprawling stems bearing pairs of oval, serrated leaves and clusters of bright pinkish-purple flowers. Likes dry sunny ground. S. Europe. Jul.-Aug. ☼ **Garden Catmint** *Nepeta* x *faassenii* (**2**) HP is a well-known plant forming hummocks, up to 45cm tall, with greyish foliage and bluish-mauve flowers. An easy plant to grow but often rather invasive, and for that reason best clipped hard back each year after flowering. Attractive to cats, though not nearly so much as the true Catmint, *N. cataria*, which drives most felines quite distracted. Jun.-Sept. ☼◑ 'Blue Beauty' - lavender-blue; 'Six Hills Giant' - taller to

3

4

60cm. **Lamb's Ear** *Stachys olympica* (= *S. lanata*) (**3**) HP is a very well-known plant, forming creeping mats of rather coarse, silvery-woolly leaves (lamb's ears). The gawky, flower stems rise to 40cm tall. Often rather invasive but producing a fine effect in the front of a border. Very easy to grow on most average, well-drained soils. W. Asia. Jul.-Sept. ☼☻ 'Silver Carpet' - non-flowering form. *S. byzantinus* is a finer plant with larger grey-green leaves. *S. macrantha* (= *Betonica grandiflora)* (**4**) HP is a handsome erect plant, up to 45cm tall, with deep green, heart-shaped leaves and large oblong clusters of rosy-purple flowers. Deserves to be more widely grown. W. Asia. Jun.-Jul. ☼☻ 'Rosea Superba' - the finest form.

1

MINT FAMILY (contd) **Obedient Plant** *Physostegia virginiana* HP is a stiffly erect, leafy plant, up to 1m tall, its deep green leaves narrow and serrated. The pointed, two-sided flower spikes are a handsome rose-pink, often branched below. Good on most average soils. The individual flowers can be pushed into any position and there they will stay, hence the common name. N. America. Jul.-Sept. ☼☾ 'Rose Bouquet' (**1**) - lilac-pink, the most popular; 'Summer Snow'; 'Summer Spire' - rose-pink, 75cm; 'Vivid' - deep rose, only 50cm. **Salvias** form a large group, much used in gardens. Some of the finest are listed here. **Meadow Salvia** *Salvia pratensis* (**2**) HP is often semi-sprawling in habit with coarse oblong leaves and

relatively large lilac-blue flowers borne in lax spikes. There are also pink and white forms. Britain (rare as a wild species) & Europe. May-Jul. ☼☾ *S. interrupta* HP is more handsome, up to 1m tall, with compound leaves, dull grey beneath, and large royal purple flowers - very striking! Requires a sheltered, well-drained site. N. Africa. Jun.-Jul. ☼ **Clary** *Salvia sclarea* (**3**) HB is a foxy-smelling plant, forming a large rosette of rough hairy, heart-shaped leaves in the first year. In the second a fairly stout, branched stem, up to 1m tall, bears numerous white or pale blue flowers, surrounded by pink or whitish bracts. Long cultivated. S. Europe & Middle East. Jun.-Aug. ☼☾

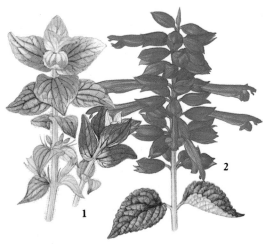

MINT FAMILY **Bluebeard** *S. horminium* (**1**) HHA is an erect, thin-stemmed plant, up to 50cm tall, with insignificant spikes of whitish flowers, each spike topped by a tuft of showy bright purple bracts. S. Europe. Jul.-Sept. ☼ 'Pink Lady' - has pink bracts; 'Bouquet Mixed' - colours from white and pink to blue and purple. **Scarlet Sage** *S. splendens* (**2**) HHA is by far, the best known and most popular Salvia in gardens with its striking brilliant scarlet flower spikes. A much-grown bedding plant for sunny sheltered places, up to 30cm tall. Brazil. Jun.-Sept. ☼ 'Carabiniere'; 'Fireball'; 'Red Hussar'; 'Royal

Mountie'; 'Dress Parade' - purple flowers. *S. argentea* HB is an erect plant, up to 70cm tall, valued for its rosettes of large, soft woolly leaves. Flowers white, on branched stems, in the second year. Mediterranean. Jun.-Aug. ☼ *Salvia* x *superba* HP, one of the very finest, forms stout erect clumps, up to 90cm high, with cramped spikes of small violet-blue flowers. Plants are best placed outdoors in the spring as rooted divisions, for young plants do not overwinter well. Jun.-Aug. ☼ 'East Friesland' - only 45cm tall; 'Lubeca' - violet-purple; 'May Night' - intense violet-purple, 45cm. **Self-Heal** *Prunella grandiflora* (**3**) is similar to *P. vulgaris*, which grows wild in Europe, though showier, forming spreading mats of oblong leaves and short stems bearing dense heads of deep violet-blue flowers. An aggressive grower but fine in poor starved places beneath hedges or on banks; easy and showy. C. & S. Europe. May-Jul. ☼☻ 'Loveliness' - lilac; 'Loveliness Pink'.

3

MINT FAMILY (contd) **Spotted Deadnettle** *Lamium maculatum* (**2**) HP is a creeping plant forming loose mats of heart-shaped leaves which frequently have white blotches in the centre. The sprawling or upright flower stems rise to 25cm with fairly large whorls of rose-purple flowers. Like Self-Heal (p.127) a fine cottage garden flower but too invasive for smaller, more ordered gardens. Both require little attention and reward one with a fine show of blooms each year. Europe & W. Asia. Apr.-Aug. ☼☻ 'Beacon Silver' (**1**) - best by far, with silvery, green-edged leaves forming a dense mat. Useful for ground cover or for a contrast of texture or colour.

3

PEA FAMILY is one of the largest and most important of all plant families with representatives in many parts of the world and including trees, climbers and herbs. Some are important food plants, many others have decorative value. **Goat's Rue** *Galega officinalis* (**3**) HP is an old cottage garden favourite, forming an erect bushy plant, up to 120cm tall, with compound leaves bearing up to 17 oblong leaflets. The mauve and whitish flowers are closely grouped in short lateral clusters. These are followed by slender straight 'pea pods'. The flowers are produced in abundance and some more richly coloured forms are listed in catalogues. C. & Europe. Jul.-Sept. ☼◖

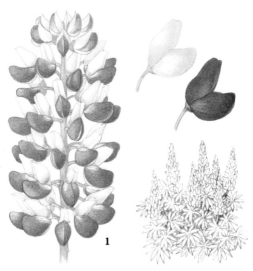

1

PEA FAMILY (contd) **Lupin** (1) HP The modern border lupins have a complex origin which has involved much breeding and selection based on hybridisation between *Lupinus arboreus* from S. Europe and *L. polyphyllus* from N. America. The Russell Lupin was the forerunner of most modern named cultivars. They are a vigorous breed, forming stout clumps up to 1m tall, with spires of closely set pea-flowers in many colours: yellow, blue, purple, pink, red or white, or often bicoloured. All require a deep, rich, well-

2

drained soil but dislike a chalky one. Numerous
varieties are listed in catalogues. Jun.-Aug. ☼
Baptisia *Baptisia australis* (**2**) HP is a handsome plant
from North America, thriving in most average garden
soils, but often taking a year or two to become
properly established. Plants form erect bushes, up to
80cm tall, with large trefoil leaves. The violet-blue
flowers are borne in rather loose, lupin-like racemes
and followed by rich-brown pea pods which are
excellent for drying. Jun.-Jul. ☼★

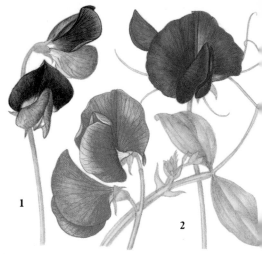

1

2

PEA FAMILY (contd) **Sweet Pea** *Lathyrus odoratus* (**2**)
HA Few plants have such an appeal. The wide range
of colours found in modern strains and the sweet
scent accompanying the flowers are rightly prized.
The wild plant (**1**) has dark purple flowers with pale
bluish-lilac 'wings' and has been cultivated since the
17th century. Seeds can be sown during the winter or
early spring under glass, or outdoors in the spring.
Sweet Peas need a rich, moist, well-drained soil with
added compost or manure. There are many named
varieties and, in addition, some modern dwarf,
non-climbing, strains such as 'Little Elfin' and

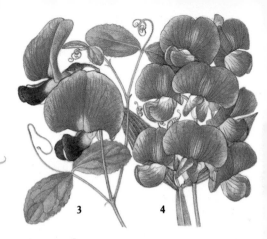

3   4

'Snoopea'. S. Italy & Sicily. Jun.-Sept. ☼△
Everlasting Pea *Lathyrus latifolius* (**4**) HP is often seen
naturalised in Britain, northern Europe and else-
where. Plants form a stout entanglement, climbing with branched tendrils to 2m. The flowers are a rich
purplish-pink and are similar to the Sweet Pea, but
smaller and thicker in texture, not scented. Easy on
most soils. C.& S. Europe. Jun.-Jul. ☼☙ 'White
Pearl'; 'Rose Queen'. *L. grandiflorus* (**3**) HP is even
finer, with slender angled stems and more rounded
leaflets. The flowers are larger, magenta-purple with
dark crimson-purple wings. A fine cottage garden
plant; excellent on fences or tree stumps. Italy &
Greece. Jul.-Aug. ☼☙

1

2

PEA FAMILY (contd) **Spring Vetching** *Lathyrus (=Orobus) vernus* (**1**) HP is a delightful spring flower, especially good in semi-shaded borders mixed with dwarf bulbs, Snowdrops, Scillas and Anemones in particular. Plants form erect tufts up to 40cm tall. The compound leaves have two to four pairs of oval leaflets. The small blue, purple or violet pea flowers are borne in one-sided clusters. Easy to grow and very graceful. Europe. Mar.-May. ☻● 'Spring Delight' - creamy-pink flowers. *L. aureus* (**2**) is similar but with dense clusters of buff-yellow flowers, but scarcely as effective. Europe. May-Jun. ☻

LILY FAMILY is a showy and important family with many bulbous and tuberous-rooted species. **African Lily** *Agapanthus campanulatus* (**3**) HHP is an imposing plant forming large tufts of broad, strap-shaped leaves. Flowers, in large umbels on stout leafless stems, up to 180cm tall. South Africa. Jul.-Sept. ☼ *A. orientalis* HHP, from the same region, is finer with more evergreen foliage and pale to deep blue flowers on stems up to 120cm tall. Jul.-Sept. ☼ Both require some winter protection in all but the mildest districts. Modern hybrids are mostly hardy and make excellent border plants. 'Blue Giant'; 'Bressingham Blue' - 70cm; 'Bressingham White' - 90cm; 'Headborne Hybrids' - blue shades, 70-90cm.

3

LILY FAMILY (contd) **Common Bluebell** *Endymion (= Hyacinthoides) non-scriptus* HP, the native plant of Britain and W. Europe, is not particularly good in gardens but a fine plant for naturalizing beneath trees. May-Jun. ☙ **Spanish Bluebell** *E. hispanicus* (**1**) HP is very much finer as a garden plant, but beware, it can become extremely invasive and the leaves are very untidy after flowering ceases. The flowers occur in stiff erect spikes, up to 50cm tall, with broader, shorter bells than the Common Bluebell, in shades of blue, pink or white. Most effective in drifts between shrubs. Spain and Portugal. May-June. ◐◑△ **Crown Imperial** *Fritillaria imperialis* HP is one of the

1

most popular and imposing of all bulbous plants. The clusters of broad, orange-red bells are borne on stout stems up to 1m tall. The large bulbs should be planted 15-20cm deep in rich, well-drained soils. W. & C. Asia. May-Jun. ☼ 'Lutea' - lemon-yellow; 'Maxima Rubra' (**2**) - deep red. **Snakeshead Fritillary** *F. meleagris* (**3**) is a native of British and W. European riverside meadows, ideal for naturalizing or as groups in the spring border. The thin stems, 30cm tall, bear a single, or two, purple-chequered lantern flowers, sometimes white. Apr.-May. ☼❂

LILY FAMILY (contd) **Hostas** or **Plantain Lilies** HP are grown primarily for their striking ribbed foliage. *Hosta lancifolia* (**1**) has young foliage of rich, glossy-green and loose racemes of lavender-blue flowers, 45cm tall. China. Jul.-Aug. ☼☽ *H. plantaginea* is similar but with glossy yellowish-green leaves and rather congested racemes of white, fragrant flowers. China. Jul.-Aug. ☽● *H. sieboldiana* (**5**) makes huge clumps, up to 70cm tall, with striking large blue-green leaves. The flowers are rather poor, pale whitish-mauve. Japan. Jun.-Jul. ☼☽ *H. fortunei* is similar to the preceding species but with narrower,

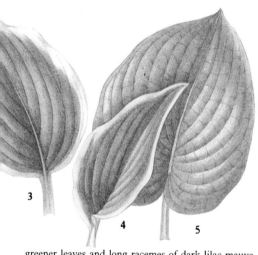

3

4

5

greener leaves and long racemes of dark lilac-mauve
flowers. China. July-August. ☼☾ 'Aurea Marginata'
(**4**) - leaves edged cream; 'Albo Picta' (= Picta) -
leaves green and yellow. *H. ventricosa* is robust, with
deep shiny green leaves. The flowers are violet-blue
drooping in long racemes. China. Jul.-Aug. ☼☾
'Aurea Maculata' - leaves blotched yellow; 'Variegata'
(**2**) - leaves with white variegations, very fine.
Three excellent hybrids are well worth growing: 'Frances
Williams' - blue-green leaves with beige variegations;
'Thomas Hoog' (**3**) - leaves large, white-edged;
'Crispula' - similar but leaves wavy.

LILY FAMILY (contd) **Day Lilies** *Hemerocallis* HP have short-lived individual flowers but produce them in profusion. The species have mostly been superceded by a host of exotic cultivars, 50-100cm tall, in a wide range of colours; flowers single (**1**) or double (**2**). *H. citrina* has sweetly scented, lemon-yellow flowers. China. Jul.-Aug. ☼☻ *H. fulva* is equally robust, up to 100cm tall, with coarser orange-yellow flowers. More drought resistant. E. Europe & W.Asia. *H. flava (= H. lilio-asphodelus)* is widespread in Europe and Asia; a lower plant with clear yellow flowers. Modern strains are complex in origin and mostly very reliable and adaptable. **Lilies** *Lilium* HP are widely grown bulbs, excellent for the herbaceous border or woodland garden. Most prefer deep moist rich cool soils. Some are liable to virus infections and only healthy reliable bulbs should be planted. The two species which follow are both lime tolerant. **Maddona Lily** *L. candidum* (**3**) is an old favourite which greatly resents disturbance. The heavily perfumed, broad white trumpets are borne on tall stems, up to 1m in height. Plant 6-10cm deep. Greece & W. Asia. July. ☼☻ **Regal Lily** *L. regale* (**4**) HP is equally popular, with deep green leaves and narrow trumpet flowers, white with a yellow centre and flushed wine-red on the reverse, and deliciously fragrant. Plant 20cm deep. China. Jul.-Aug. ☼☻△

3

4

LILY FAMILY (contd) **Pyrenean Lily** *Lilium pyrenaicum* (**1**) bears charming small yellow 'turkscap' flowers on stems 70cm tall but is rather evil smelling. There is also an orange form. Pyrenees. Jun.-Jul. ☼☽ **Tiger Lily** *L. tigrinum* (**3**) is taller, with large 'turkscaps,' orange-red with purple spots. Easy to grow and very fine. The leaves bear small bulbils in their axils which can be grown on. China & Japan.

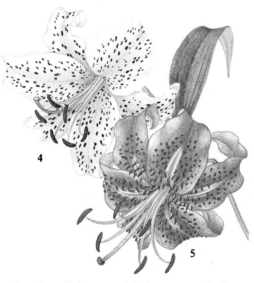

4

5

Aug.-Sept. ☙ **Martagon Lily** *L. martagon* (**2**), 80cm
tall, its lower leaves in distinct whorls, has small dull
purple 'turkscaps'. Europe. Jul.-Aug. ☙ 'Album' -
white flowers. **Golden-rayed Lily** *L. auratum* (**4**) is
superb, up to 2m tall, carrying large, beautifully-
scented flowers. Requires lime-free soil. Japan.
Jul.-Aug. ☙ *L. speciosum* (**5**), rarely over 1.2m, has
large flowers with reflexed petals. Plant bulbs at least
20cm deep in lime-free soil. Japan. Aug.-Sept. ☙☙

143

LILY FAMILY (contd) **Onions** *Allium* HP, a large genus of bulbous plants distributed across most of the northern hemisphere, includes a number of highly ornamental species and the well-known culinary onion, shallot, garlic and chives. Most of the decorative species thrive in a well-drained soil in full sun. The majority have a strong onion smell, so do not make good cut flowers, but the dried fruit heads do not usually smell and are excellent for indoor decoration. *A. afflatunense* (**2**), 1m tall, has medium-

4   5

sized heads of lilac-purple flowers. USSR. May-Jun.
☼★ *A. christophii* (= *A. albopilosum*) (**1**), 40cm, has
massive heads of metallic-purple, starry flowers, very
fine. USSR. Jun.-Jul. ☼★ *A. sphaerocephalum* (**3**),
75cm, has small, dense, deep violet-purple flowers.
S. Europe. Jun.-Jul. ☼★ **Yellow Garlic** *A. moly* (**5**)
is widely grown and often spreads rapidly in gardens.
Plants grow up to 30cm tall. S. Europe. Jun. ☼ *A.
siculum* (**4**) has rather untidy leaves and a stout stem
carrying a loose head of drooping green and pink
bells, which become upright in fruit. E. Europe & W.
Asia. Jun.-Jul. ☼★

145

LILY FAMILY (contd) **Lily of the Valley** *Convallaria majalis* (**1**) HP forms low spreading carpets of deep green oval leaves. Half hidden amongst these arise the arching racemes of white, deliciously scented flowers, followed by small red berries. Europe. Apr.-May. ☾● 'Fortin's Giant' - the best white; 'Rubra' - pink flowers, less effective. **Liriope** *L. muscari* (**2**) HP is a tough plant forming deep green grassy tussocks, 30cm tall. The small violet-mauve flowers are borne in dense spikes. Useful ground cover below shrubs or in dark corners. N. America. Aug.-Nov. ☾ **Red Hot Pokers** *Knifophia* (**3**) HP-HHP are flamboyant plants

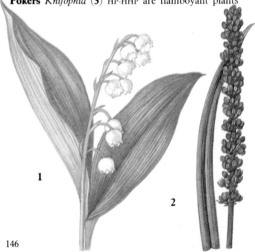

1

2

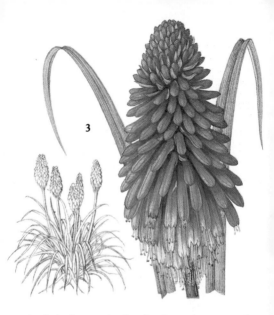

for the herbaceous border, forming coarse green tufts of sword-like leaves. The stout flower spikes (pokers) rise 60-120cm, carrying numerous tubular flaming red or yellow flowers. A plant for rich soils in sunny sheltered places. S. Africa (Cape). Jul.-Sept. ☼ *K. galpinii* HHP is altogether more refined, 60cm tall, with small bright yellow or orange pokers. S. Africa. Jul.-Sept. ☼

LILY FAMILY (contd) **Tulips** *Tulipa* HP *T. praestans* (**1**) is one of the easiest to grow of this popular group of bulbous plants, 30cm tall, each stem carrying up to four orange-red flowers. S. USSR. Apr. ☼ *T. tarda* (**2**), only 8cm tall, has small starry flowers, white with a yellow centre. Very floriferous. S. USSR. Apr. ☼ **Lady Tulip** *T. clusiana* is an old favourite, 40cm tall, with white flowers stained red on the outside. Middle East. May. ☼ Var. *chrysantha* has yellow and red blooms (**3**). *T. greigii* (**6**) has many forms. Most grow

4

5

6

to about 39cm tall with attractive dark striped or spotted leaves and relatively large yellow or red flowers. S. USSR. Apr. ☼ The huge range of widely grown garden tulips are divided into many sections. The best-known are the Darwin and Cottage Garden types (**4**), the Parrot Tulips, with their ragged petals, the Lily-flowered Tulips (**5**), with slender pointed petals. Many are excellent for bold bedding schemes and for cutting. Consult detailed bulb catalogues when choosing which to grow.

LILY FAMILY (contd) **Solomon's Seals** *Polygonatum*
HP are a distinguished group of plants, grown easily,
but for their elegant growth rather than their flowers.
They prefer a deep, moist soil. **Common Solomon's
Seal** *P. multiflorum* (**1**), has graceful arching stems,
80cm tall, bearing soft, blue-green, oval leaves with
oblong greenish-white flowers hung beneath in twos
and threes. Europe. May-Jul.✿● *P. roseum* is
similar, the leaves more crowded and the flowers pale
pink. N. Asia. *V. verticillatum* (**2**) is easily disting-

uished by its erect stems, often 1m tall, and whorls of slender leaves and clusters of small greenish flowers. Asia. Jun.-Jul. ☽● *P. comutatum* is a fine plant, sometimes available, with broad shiny foliage on 70-80cm stems. USA. May-Jun. *P. japonicum* is perhaps the largest species cultivated, up to 100cm, though not far removed from *P. multiflorum*. Japan. May-Jun. ☽●

LIMNANTHES FAMILY contains only a single species in general cultivation. **Poached Egg Flower** *Limnanthes douglasii* (**3**) HA is a gay tufted plant, often rather sprawling, up to 15cm tall, with bright green, cut foliage. The solitary flowers are bright yellow edged with white, although sometimes plain yellow. Excellent for bees. Seed can be sown in the spring, or in late summer to flower the following year. An easy and bright little annual, often seeding itself around. W. USA. Jun.-Aug. ☼☽

3

FLAX FAMILY is the family that contains Linen and Linseed, both varieties of *Linum usitatissimum*. **Yellow Flax** *L. flavum* (**3**) HP reaches 30cm tall or more, with grey-green leaves and sprays of yellow flowers. C. & S. Europe. Jun.-Aug. ☼ **Crimson Flax** *L. grandiflorum* (**2**) HA grows erect to 30cm high with narrow green leaves and glowing crimson flowers with a black centre. Algeria. Jul.-Sept. ☼ *L. narbonense* (**1**) HP grows up to 50cm tall, with small grey-green leaves and panicles of delightful bright sky-blue flowers. W. & S. Europe. Jun.-Sept. ☼

4

LOASA FAMILY is primarily an American family of annual and perennial herbs, often with savage stinging hairs. The following species, however, is quite harmless. **Bartonia** *Mentzelia lindleyi* (= *Bartonia aurea*) (**4**) HA is an erect branched herb, up to 60cm tall, with narrow, lobed leaves. The relatively large flowers are rather mallow-like but bright yellow, their centres often stained with crimson or orange, each petal drawn to a short point. A bright and cheerful annual for a sheltered warm border. California. Jun.-Sept. ☼

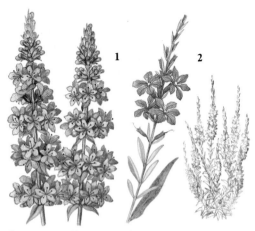

LOOSESTRIFE FAMILY is a family of mainly tropical plants but with a number of showy representatives in temperate regions. **Purple Loosestrife** *Lythrum salicaria* (**1**) HP is an erect bushy herb 70-120cm tall, with four-angled, hairy stems and narrow, lance-shaped leaves, often in whorls. The magenta-purple flowers form long spikes. A plant for moist soils. Europe. Jul.-Sept. ☼☻ 'Beacon' - rosy-purple; 'Firecandle' - rose-red; 'Lady Sackville' - purple; 'Robert' - clear pink. *L. virgatum* (**2**) HP is similar but with more slender hairless stems, paired willow-like leaves and spikes of rose-pink flowers. C. & E. Europe. Jul.-Sept. ☼☻ 'The Rocket' - rose-red; 'Rose-Queen' - perhaps the finest.

MALLOW FAMILY is a large and widespread family of trees, shrubs and herbs, containing some popular garden plants. **Hollyhock** *Althaea rosea* (**3**) HP is a favourite old cottage garden flower, though less planted today than it deserves. Plants may reach up to 2m tall with long spikes of mallow blooms, double or single, in shades of crimson, pink, maroon, mauve or white. Hollyhock Rust can devastate plants in some areas, although seed-raised plants are often less susceptible. W. Asia. Jul.-Sept. A number of named strains are available from seedsmen including 'Marjorette' - only 60cm tall. *A. ficifolia*, with more deeply lobed leaves and sulphur-yellow flowers, has been hybridized with *A. rosea* to produce yellow, apricot and salmon offspring.

3

MALLOW FAMILY (contd) **Shrubby Mallow** *Lavatera olbia* (**1**) HP is a subshrubby plant, 1-3m tall, with grey-felted leaves and stems bearing rose-pink flowers. Striking at the back of the border or as a feature on its own. Mediterranean. Jul.-Oct. ☼
Lavatera *Lavatera trimestris* (**2**)HA is a colourful plant with erect stems, up to 80cm tall, bearing large mallow-blooms with satiny petals in pink or white. S. Europe. Jul.-Sept. ☼△ 'Silver Cup' - rose-pink shaded with silver; 'Mont Blanc' - the best white, only 60cm tall. **Malope** *Malope trifida* (**3**) HHA is an erect branched herb, up to 70cm tall, with showy

crimson-purple, pink or white, satiny blooms. Handsome and easily grown, it prefers dry sunny summers. Spain. Jul.-Sept. ☼ **Sidalcea** *Sidalcea malviflora* is a widely grown mallow-like plant up to 1m tall. The lower leaves are scarcely lobed whilst the upper are dissected into narrow segments. The relatively small mauve or crimson flowers are borne in long spikes. Most named cultivars are derived from hybrids with *S. candida*. W. North America. Jun.-Aug. ☼☻ 'Croftway Red' - deep crimson-red; 'Loveliness' - shell pink; 'Mrs Anderson'- large rose-pink flowers; 'Rose-Queen' (**4**) - rose-pink.

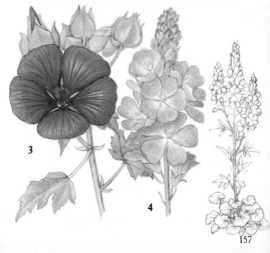

3

4

WILLLOWHERB FAMILY is a widespread family of annual and perennial herbs, often with showy, short-lived flowers, but produced in profusion. **Clarkia** Two species are commonly grown, both from North America. *Clarkia unguiculata (= C. elegans)* HA is a slender plant, 40-120cm tall, with oval leaves and rosy-purple flowers. *C. pulchella* is lower growing, rarely more than 30cm high, with narrow leaves and purple flowers. Modern strains, however, bear little resemblance to their parents and occur in a wide range of exciting colours (**1**): pink, purple, salmon, crimson, scarlet and mauve, besides white. Double forms are also available. Aug.-Oct. ☼☻△

2

Evening Primrose *Oenothera* is a North American group of annual or perennial herbs, generally with large four-petalled flowers, opening in the evening or on dull days. *O. erythrosepala* HB is robust, up to 1.2m tall, with lance-shaped leaves and pale yellow flowers with red-tipped petals. Jun.-Aug. ☼◑ *O. missouriensis* (**2**) HHP is rather sprawling, with narrow untoothed leaves and large yellow flowers, which flush with pink or red as they age. Dislikes wet winters. Jun.-Aug. ☼ *O. speciosa* HHP is the finest, an erect plant, up to 60cm tall, with large white flowers, fading to pink. Jul.-Sept. ☼ There are some fine cultivars of hybrid origin: 'Fireworks'- 45cm, purplish-green leaves, bright yellow flowers; 'Highlight' - 60cm, prolific, yellow; 'Yellow River' - 40cm, rich yellow.

1

WILLOWHERB FAMILY (contd) **Zauschneria** *Zauschneria californica* (**1**) HHP is a most striking subshrubby plant of rather loose growth, 30-60cm tall, with oblong leaves, either opposite or alternate on the stem. The solitary flowers are bright scarlet, rather the shape of a *Clarkia* bloom. The seeds are plumed like those of Willowherb. Unfortunately this lovely plant is not reliably hardy in northern temperate climates, however, cuttings can be easily overwintered in a protected place and planted out in late spring. Apart from this it is an easy plant to grow on most ordinary well-drained soils. Give it as much sun as possible. California. Jul.-Sept. ☼

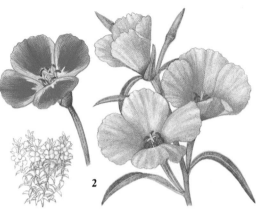

2

Godetia HA is a popular garden annual of rather obscure origin, but thought to have come from a Californian species *Godetia amoena* (**2**). Botanists mostly lump *Godetia* into *Clarkia*, though in gardens the two look quite distinct. Plants grow rather stiffly, 30-60cm tall, with oval leaves and stems topped by short spikes of large satiny flowers, like small Evening Primroses, in shades of pink, crimson, salmon purple, mauve or sometimes white. Double and single-flowered forms occur. Most modern strains are compact and seedsmen generally offer mixed colours in both tall and dwarf forms. They are easy to grow on most average soils. Jun.-Sept. ☼△ 'Kelvedon Glory' - lush salmon-orange flowers; 'Sybil Sherwood' - salmon-pink flowers.

1

2

POPPY FAMILY is a relatively large family distributed throughout the globe, but the largest number are from the temperate northern hemisphere. **Bleeding Heart** *Dicentra spectabilis* (**2**) HP is an elegant plant, up to 60cm tall, with ferny green foliage and nodding racemes of heart-shaped flowers, bright rose-pink with a white middle. Although hardy, the shoots can be nipped by spring frosts. N. China. May-Jul. ☺● 'Alba' - ivory flowers. *D. eximea* forms low tufts, up to 20cm tall, of grey-green, finely cut leaves beset with arching racemes of purplish-pink flowers. E. USA. May-Aug. ☺ 'Spring Morning' -

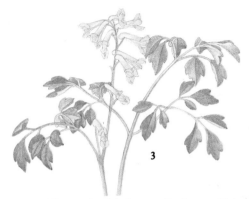

3

50cm, delicate pale pink flowers. *D. formosa* (**1**) is closely related and widely grown and has shorter flowers. W. USA. Hybrids between the last two species have been recorded: 'Luxuriant' - 30cm, with bright red flowers, is the finest. **Corydalis** *Corydalis lutea* (**3**) HP is widely grown, indeed it is often found naturalized on steps and in walls in some areas. Plants form mounds of blue-green, fragile, ferny foliage, up to 25cm high, dotted through the spring and summer by dense racemes of bright yellow flowers. A charming plant, perhaps seen at its best on a dry stone wall. Europe. May-Sept. ☙● *C. cheilanthifolia* is more robust with fine ferny leaves and racemes of dull yellow flowers. Perhaps best for its foliage and, like the previous species, revelling in moist shaded corners. China. June-July. ☙●

POPPY FAMILY (contd) **Plume Poppy** *Macleaya cordata* HP is a rather unpoppy-like plant with stout stems, up to 2m tall, sometimes more, with large alternate, hand-like, grey-green leaves. The flowers are rather insignificant, but borne in large branched panicles to give a broad plume of white which is most effective at a distance. An easy plant to grow, and best at the back of an herbaceous border. China and Japan. Jul.-Sept. ☼ 'Kelway's Coral Plume' (**1**) - a fine variety with misty-pink flowers. It is probably a form of the closely related *M. microcarpa*.

2

Californian Poppy *Eschscholtzia californica* (**2**) HA is a
cheerful and popular annual, easily grown from seed
and often overwintering in milder districts. Plants are
rather sprawling with pale whitish stems and finely
cut grey-green leaves. The solitary flowers are borne
on long stalks, the green calyx popping off like a little
cap as they open. The satiny petals come in many
colours, white, cream, yellow, orange, red, pink or
bronze. There are both single and semi-double forms.
Flowers are short-lived when cut. California. Jun.-
Sept. ☼△ 'Ballerina' - a fine selection of semi-double
mixed colours. Although single colours are sold,
seedsmen generally offer a mixture.

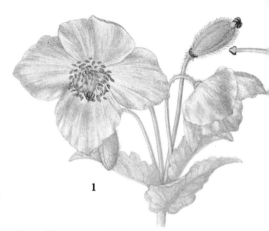

1

POPPY FAMILY (contd) **Blue Poppy** *Meconopsis* These justly famous plants are amongst the most exquisite of all garden flowers. They relish moist peaty soils. **Himalayan Blue Poppy** *M. betonicifolia* (= *M. baileyi*) (**1**) HB, the most famous of all, has bristly, oblong, matt green leaves and erect slender stems, growing to 90cm tall, on which the superb large flowers half nod. The almost transparent petals are pure blue in the best forms, with a hint of lavender or violet in others. S.W. China. Jun.-Jul. ☙ *M. grandis* HP has even larger and bluer flowers, sometimes red or purple, but is less easy to please. The hybrids such as 'Branklyn' are equally fine and, if anything, better garden plants and reliably perennial in habit. **Horned**

2

3

Poppy *Glaucium flavum* (**2**) HP is a wild plant of
shingle shorelines which grows well in cultivation,
given a sunny spot and a well-drained soil. Plants
form a basal rosette of crinkly, lobed, blue-green
leaves. Smooth stems, 80cm tall, carry yellow
poppies. Europe & W. Asia. Jul.-Sept. ☼ *G.
corniculatum* is similar but more robust and with deep
orange-red flowers. **Welsh Poppy** *Meconopsis cam-
brica* (**3**) HP forms a basal tuft of lobed yellowish-green
leaves with stems up to 40cm high bearing small
poppy flowers in clear yellow or orange. S.W.
Europe. Jun.-Aug. ☻

POPPY FAMILY **Poppies** *Papaver* Many different poppies are cultivated but there is space here for a selection only. **Common Poppy** *P. rhoeas* (**1**) HA The wild poppy of the arable fields of Europe, with its bright scarlet flowers, is now sadly a scarce sight in the landscape. The 'Shirley Strains' are selections with both single and double flowers in shades of pink, red and orange, as well as white. Europe. Jun.-Aug.

☼ **Opium Poppy** *P. somniferum* (**3**) HA is a favourite cottage garden flower. Plants are stiff and upright with crinkly grey-green fleshy leaves and large white, purple or red flowers, followed by attractive seed-pods. Double forms are offered by seedsmen,

including both 'Carnation' and 'Paeony' strains (**2**).
Middle East. Jun.-Aug. ☼ **Oriental Poppies** (**4**) HP
The splendid bold summer poppies of our gardens
are derived from two species, *Papaver orientale* and *P.
bracteatum*, both natives of West Asia. They are
amongst the most brazen of all garden flowers. Most
form tough dense tussocks of bristly leaves. The
flowering stems, 60-120cm tall, bear a single flower,
brilliant scarlet in the wild type. May-Jun. ☼ 'Black
and White' - white with a black centre; 'Cedric's
Pink' - pure clear pink with a black centre; 'Goliath'
- crimson-scarlet with a black centre; 'Mrs Stobart' -
cerise; 'Mrs Perry' - salmon-pink with a black centre;
'Picotee' - frilly white flowers edged with salmon.

4

PLUMBAGO FAMILY is an Old World family, primarily
of arid and saline regions. **Thrift** *Armeria maritima* HP
forms deep-green cushions of slender leaves. The
pink flowerheads are borne on long leafless stems.
Europe. Jun.-Aug. ☼☕ 'Dusseldorf' - 15cm, red;
'Ruby Glow' - 25cm; 'Vindictive' - 10cm, deep rose.
A. pseudarmeria (**1**) is more robust, with tufts of
strap-shaped leaves and rose-pink flowerheads on
long stems, 30-60cm tall. Spain, Portugal & N.
Africa. Jun.-Aug. ☼ 'Bees' Ruby' - the finest
cultivar. **Ceratostigma** *Ceratostigma plumbaginoides*
(**2**) HP is a sprawling plant, up to 30cm tall, with
stringy stems, rounded leaves and purple flowers with
deep blue lobes. China. Sept.-Nov. ☼☕

1

2

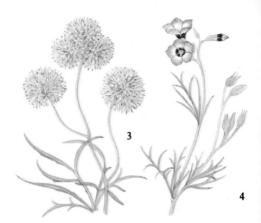

PHLOX FAMILY is a small family of annual and perennial herbs, primarily American in origin. **Gilia** *Gilia achilleifolia* (**3**) HHA grows up to 30cm, the leaves with slender segments and the violet-blue flowers borne in tight scabious-like clusters. California. Jul.-Aug. ☼ *G. capitata* is similar, but smaller, with richer violet flowers. California. Jul.-Aug. ☼ *A. rubra* HHB is undoubtedly the finest, though unreliable in northern climates it is well worth trying. Plants have stiff stems, up to 90cm tall, bearing brilliant sealing-wax flowers. S. USA and Mexico. Jun.-Aug. ☼ *G. tricolor* (**4**) HA is the easiest to grow, only 30cm tall, with thin-lobed leaves and violet-blue flowers, darker in the throat and with a yellow or orange tube. California. Jul.-Sept. ☼

PHLOX FAMILY (contd) **Jacob's Ladder** *Polemonium caeruleum* (**1**) HP is a variable plant, forming tufts with erect stems, up to 90cm tall. The distinctive pinnate leaves give the plant its common name. It is widely distributed as a wild plant in the cooler parts of the northern hemisphere. The pale to dark blue, cup-shaped flowers are borne in dense clusters. An easy plant to grow on most soils, often seeding itself around. May-Jun. ☼☽ 'Blue Pearl' - 25cm; 'Sapphire' - 35cm, pale blue; 'Pink Beauty' - 35cm, pinkish-purple. *P. foliosissimum*, 75cm tall with lavender-blue flowers and closely allied to *P. caeruleum*, is in many ways a finer plant and not nearly so invasive in gardens.

Linanthus (often included in *Gilia* or *Leptosiphon*) are charming annuals, easily recognised by their whorls of fine leaves and rather starry, though bluntpetalled, flowers. They are easy to grow in most soils in a warm sunny position. *Linanthus grandiflorus* (**3**) HA has a slender habit, up to 25cm tall, with pale lavender or white flowers in dense terminal clusters. California. Jun.-Jul. ☼ *G. androsaceus* (**2**) is similar but with flowers in yellow, orange, lavender or pink shades. W. USA. Jun.-Jul. Hybrids between these (*L. x hybridus*) are often offered in seed catalogues. These are lovely dwarfs, often only 8cm tall, with flowers in all shades except blue. Delightful at the front of a border or for dull corners on the rock garden.

PHLOX FAMILY (contd) **Phloxes** are widely grown and popular herbaceous border flowers flowering in late summer. **Annual Phlox** *Phlox drummondii* (**1**) HHA is a delightful plant that deserves to be more widely grown, especially for its bright flowers and long season. Plants form erect tufts up to 30cm tall, with hairy stems and oblong leaves. The flowers are borne in dense clusters, blue, purple, red, crimson or white, often with a paler or darker 'eye'. Most forms have rather rounded petals. S. USA. Jul.-Oct. ☼ 'Twinkles' - a remarkable strain with star-shaped flowers, the petals pointed rather than rounded. **Border Phloxes** (**2**) HP have been derived from two species from North

2

America, *P. maculata* and *P. paniculata*. They are mostly vigorous and easy to grow perennials, forming large tufts eventually. The erect stiff stems are generally between 70-100cm tall. The range of flower colours is enormous, lilac, pink, purple, mauve, carmine and white shades predominating, mostly with a pleasing fragrance. They are easy on rich moist soils and dislike midday sun. There are many named varieties. Aug.-Oct. ☼❂ 'Brigadier' - 90cm, scarlet-salmon; 'Cherry Pink' - 90cm, carmine; 'Fujiyama' - 75cm, pure white; 'Harlequin' - 75cm, variegated leaves and purple flowers; 'Mother of Pearl' - 75cm, white tinged pink; 'Prince of Orange' - 90cm, orange-salmon; 'Red Indian' - 90cm, deep crimson.

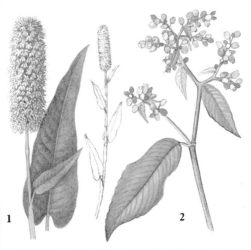

1   2

KNOTWEED FAMILY is a widespread family containing
many weedy species. Only a handful are worth
cultivating. Those described prefer moist soils. *Poly-
gonum bistorta* HP forms spreading leafy clumps with
long oval green leaves and orchid-like spikes of clear
pink flowers on stems up to 70cm tall. Europe and W.
Asia. May-Aug. ☼◐ 'Superbum' (**1**) - the finest form.
P. amplexicaule HP reaches 1m or more, with heart-
shaped leaves and spikes of red flowers. Himalaya.
Jul.-Sept. ☼◐ 'Atrosanguineum' - vivid red flowers.
P. campanulatum (**2**) HP is an altogether laxer plant,
often rather invasive, up to 80cm tall. The oval leaves

are green above, grey-tufted beneath. The small flowers form branched hazy pink sprays. Very effective planted by water. Himalaya. Aug.-Sept. ☕

PURSLANE FAMILY forms a small group of herbs or subshrubs with fleshy stems and leaves, allied to the Pink family. The *Lewisia* is perhaps the most widely grown genus, but not particularly easy to cultivate. **Portulaca** *Portulaca grandiflora* (**3**) HHA is a striking, although rather sprawling, plant with fleshy slender leaves. The solitary flowers are relatively large with five satiny petals: yellow, pink or crimson, surrounding a large bunch of stamens. A gay annual for a sunny, sheltered spot. There are double forms available as well as a single white (var. *albiflora*). The flowers are short-lived but produced in profusion over quite a long season. E. South America. Jul.-Sept. ☼

3

PRIMROSE FAMILY is a popular and rather diverse family of herbs with many cultivated species. **Cyclamen** HP has several hardy species with underground tubers, reasonably easy to grow and charming in flower. They relish a moist humus-rich soil. **Ivy-leaved Cyclamen** *Cyclamen hederifolium* (**1**) flowers in the autumn, the leaves unfurling as the pink, purple or white flowers fade. The ivy-like foliage is marbled and lasts until the early summer. S. Europe. Sept.-Nov. ☼ *C. coum* (**2**) flowers in midwinter, together with the fully developed leaves. The squat flowers are deep magenta, pink or white. W. Asia. Jan.-Mar. ☼☼ *C. repandum* (**3**) flowers in the spring together with its leaves. The flowers are deep magenta-pink and beautifully scented. S.E. Europe. Mar.-Apr. ☼ **Loosestrifes** *Lysimachia* HP No spectacular beauties can be claimed for this genus

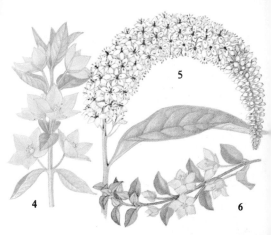

but it does contain a number of charming, garden-worthy plants. *L. clethroides* (**5**) is one of the best, forming large clumps up to 90cm tall with broad oval leaves and small white flowers crowded in curved spikes. China & Japan. Aug.-Sept. ☼☽ **Yellow Loosestrife** *L. punctata* (**4**) is a familiar cottage garden flower growing in most soil types. It forms large clumps with stiff stems, up to 90cm tall, bearing distinctive whorls of dull green leaves and starry yellow flowers. Europe & W. Asia. Jun.-Aug. ☼☽ **Creeping Jenny** *L. nummularia* (**6**) creeps over the ground, bearing pairs of rounded leaves and small starry yellow flowers. A plant for moist places. Europe. Jun.-Sept. ☽● 'Aurea' - has golden leaves.

PRIMROSE FAMILY (contd) **Primulas** HP are some of the most glorious of all our garden plants. Most of those commonly grown are plants for cool, moist, peaty soil and dislike strong sunshine. **Primrose** *Primula vulgaris* (**1**) is one of the most popular, widely cultivated and usually seeding itself around freely. Yellow is the commonest colour, but pink, blue, mauve and red and white can also be acquired. Europe & W. Asia. Mar.-May. ☼●△ **Cowslip** *P. veris* is also well-known as a wild plant. Yellow is the usual colour but both orange and red are now available. Europe. May-Jun. ☼☻△ Hybrids be-

3

tween these two have given rise to the **Polyanthus** (**2**) in a multitude of lovely colours. One of the very best of all spring bedding plants, Polyanthus are best divided every two or three years to maintain vigour. **Auricula** *P. auricula* (**3**) is often considered an old-fashioned plant but has staged something of a comeback in recent years. However, not everyone finds it an easy plant to grow and certainly it requires attention in the form of regular divisions each year after flowering. The relatively large flowers are borne in clusters on a common stalk, the colour ranging from white and yellow to rich velvety reds, browns and purples, often with contrasting bands of colour. Nurseries and seedsmen offer mixed collections or named varieties. C. Europe. Apr.-Jul. ☻

PRIMROSE FAMILY (contd) *Primula florindae* (**2**) is a
robust species, up to 80cm tall, forming large tufts.
The flowers are borne in dense terminal clusters, each
drooping on slender stalks, pale sulphurous yellow,
cowslip-scented. E. Himalaya. Jun.-Aug. ◑◯
Drumstick Primula *P. denticulata* (**1**) is one of the
easiest and most popular. A neat plant, up to 20cm
tall, with narrow oblong leaves and tight round heads
of flowers, lilac, mauve, purple, crimson or white.
Himalaya. Apr.-May. Many fine varieties such as
'Alba'; 'Bressingham Beauty' - powder blue; 'Rubin'
- red. **Candelabra Primula** *P. japonica* (**3**) HP is a
robust plant, up to 70cm tall, with coarse rosettes of

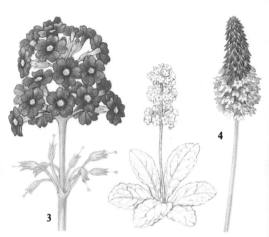

leaves. The flowers are borne in several distinct whorls on stiff stems, white, pink, purple or crimson. A popular plant, it requires ample moisture to succeed. Japan. May-Jul. ☻ 'Millers Crimson' - the best red; 'Postford White' - a fine pure white. *P. sieboldii* is a handsome plant with lax clusters of large white, lilac or rose flowers borne on a common stem. Japan & Korea. Apr.-May. ☻ 'Geisha Girl' - deep pink; 'Mikado' - rosy-magenta; 'Snowflakes' - white, very fine. *P. vialii*(**4**) is a delightful oddity with orchid-like spikes of flowers, red in bud but lavender or violet-blue when open. Attracts attention but short-lived in cultivation. W. China. Jun.-Jul. ☻

1   2   3

BUTTERCUP FAMILY is a large and cosmopolitan
family with numerous species grown in gardens.
Windflowers *Anemone* HP are charming and popular
plants succeeding on most soil types and mostly
preferring some shade. **Wood Anemone** *A. nemorosa*
(**3**) is a widespread European native, useful in gardens
beneath trees and shrubs. The ordinary form has
single white flowers. W. Europe. Mar.-Apr. ☻ 'Alba
Plena' - double flowers. *A. blanda* (**1**) is similar but
with bright azure-blue, pink or white flowers. S.
Europe. Apr.-May. ☼☻ *A. coronaria* (**2**) is the
florist's anemone, one of the most popular of all cut
flowers. Plants have single or double, poppy-like
flowers red, purple, mauve and white. Mediterranean. Mar.-Nov. ☼△ 'De Caen' - single; 'St

4

5

Brigid' - semi-double flowers. **Japanese Anemone** *A.* x *hybrida* HP is a hybrid between the Chinese *A. hupehensis* and the Himalayan *A. vitifolia* which has been cultivated for well over a century. Plants form tough spreading patches. The flowering stems are stiff, rising up to 1m tall, and bearing single or semi-double, white, pink or carmine flowers. Aug.-Nov. ☽● 'Lady Gilmour' - 60cm, double pure pink; 'September Charm' (**4**) - 45cm, soft pink, single; 'White Queen' (**5**) - 1m, white, semi-double.

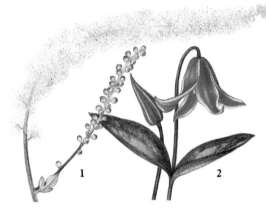

BUTTERCUP FAMILY (contd) **Bugbane** *Cimicifuga simplex* (**1**) HP is a most charming plant with elegant, thrice-divided leaves and wand-like racemes of fluffy, creamy-white flowers, up to 1m in height. A plant for moist, semi-shaded places. Temperate Asia. Aug.-Oct. ☼ 'White Pearl' - the best cultivar. *Clematis integrifolia* HP is by far the best of the herbaceous species, forming lax clumps, 45cm high. The simple stems bear single, pendent, blue or purplish, bell-shaped blooms. Europe & Asia. Jun.-Aug. ☼ 'Hendersonii' (**2**) - deep blue flowers. **Buttercups** *Ranunculus* **Fair Maids of France** *R. aconitifolius* HP is an old cottage garden plant, 90cm tall with numerous small white flowers. Europe. May-Aug.

3

4

5

☼☽ 'Plenus' - double, the usual form seen. *R. acris* 'Flore-plena' (**4**) HP is the double form of the European wild field Buttercup, often seen in gardens. May-Jul. ☼ *R. asiaticus* (**3**) HHP is the most beautiful of all the Buttercups, but not always easy to please. The flowering stems rise to 35cm, bearing large poppy-like flowers, often double, in subtle shades of pink, red, yellow or white. Needs a warm site. E. Mediterranean. June-Aug. ☼△ **Globeflower** *Trollius europaeus* HP is native to Europe. The stems, up to 75cm tall, bear large yellow or orange globe flowers. Moist soils. Europe. May-Jul. ☽ 'Canary Bird'; 'Earliest of All' (**5**) - clear yellow; 'Fireglobe' - deep orange; 'Superbus' - clear pale yellow.

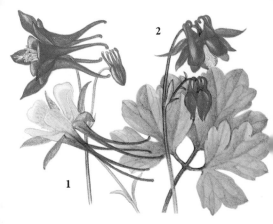

BUTTERCUP FAMILY (contd) **Columbines** *Aquilegia* HP are enchanting plants, generally easy to grow but hybridizing readily and seeding in profusion in most gardens. *A. vulgaris* (**2**), grows to 90cm tall. The nodding, spurred, flowers are in shades of pink and blue or white. Double forms exist in many old gardens. Europe. May-July. ☙ The long-spurred Columbines (**1**) are mainly hybrids of two North American species, *A. chrysantha* and *A. coerulea*. They are graceful and easy plants for well-drained soils, up to 90cm tall. Seedsmen usually offer a good mixed selection. Jun.-Aug. ☀☙ **Delphinium** HP, a noble plant, is easily raised from seed, though the best colour forms are preferably increased by division

3

or cuttings. The Garden Delphinium *D. x cultorum* (**3**) is believed to have arisen through various European and Asian species, *D. cheilanthum*, *D. grandiflorum* and *D. elatum* in particular. Plants form stout clumps with lobed leaves and spires of flowers in blues, purples, pinks, mauves and white, mostly 1-2m tall. Protect young shoots from slugs. Jun.-Aug. ☼☽ The numerous named cultivars include 'Blue Bees'; 'Black Knight' - dark blue-black; 'Blue Jay' - lilac with a white eye; 'Galahad' - white; 'Wendy' - dark blue. Nurserymen often offer a wide selection.

BUTTERCUP FAMILY (contd) **Larkspurs** *Consolida* HA
are very like *Delphinium* but annual and generally
daintier. They are easy plants for light well-drained
soils, seeding around freely in some gardens. The two
common species cultivated are *C. ambiguum* and *C.
orientalis* (**2**), both laxly branched herbs with finely
cut leaves and deep blue, spurred flowers. Modern
varieties (**1**) are more substantial with spikes of
flowers up to 90cm tall, both single and double, in
shades of blue, purple, red and pink as well as white.
The taller strains are excellent for cutting. S. Europe
& W. Asia. Jun.-Sept. ☼△

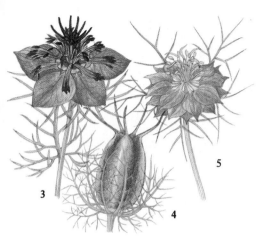

Love-in-a-Mist *Nigella damascena* (**5**) is a favourite
and very lovely cottage garden annual. Plants are
erect to 50cm with numerous finely divided, feathery
green leaves. The solitary flowers are blue or whitish
and are followed by inflated fruit capsules (**4**) which
are good for drying. Seed can also be sown in
September for early flowers the following year. S.
Europe. July-Sept. ☼△★ 'Miss Jekyll' - the finest
blue; 'Persian Jewels' - a mixture of colours including
blue, pink, red, purple and white. *N. hispanica* (**3**) is
less hardy, with purple-blue flowers. The fruit pods
are less obviously inflated. S. Spain & N. Africa.
Jul.-Aug. ☼

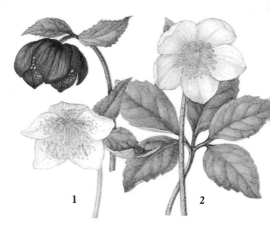

1

2

BUTTERCUP FAMILY (contd) *Helleborus* is a handsome and popular genus with striking foliage and large but subtle flowers. **Christmas Rose** *H. niger* (**2**) is a much sought after plant, though not always the easiest to grow and greatly resenting disturbance of any sort. The white, saucer flowers are of great beauty. Hates dry soils. Europe. Feb.-Apr. ☙△ **Lenten Rose** *H. orientalis* x *H. atrorubens* (**1**) is similar but forming taller more substantial clumps. The flowers are relatively small but occur in an exciting range of colours from white to greenish and pink to the deepest plum-purple. They all thrive in rich deep soils. W. Asia. Feb.-May. ☙△ *Helleborus argutifolius* (*H. corsicus* of gardens) (**4**) is a most handsome

evergreen plant with stout stems up to 60cm tall, bearing large shiny, prickly-edged, three-parted leaves. Early in the year a large cluster of apple-green blooms emerges from the stem tops. Corsica & Sardinia. Feb.-May. ☻☼ **Stinking Hellebore** *H. foetidus* (**3**), is a handsome, though foetid, plant, fine for naturalizing in woodland or between shrubs. The deep green fingery leaves are a perfect foil for the small, paler, maroon-edged, bell-shaped flowers. W. Europe. Mar.-May. ☻☼

BUTTERCUP FAMILY (contd) **Meadow Rues** *Thalictrum* HP is a genus of relatively unspectacular plants. However, two at least are well worth growing. *T. aquilegifolium* (**1**) is a stout erect plant, up to 120cm tall, with ferny leaves and large massed heads of fluffy rosy-purple flowers consisting mostly of stamens. Easily grown. Europe & Asia. May-Jun. ☼☽ 'Album' - attractive whitish flowers. *T. dipterocarpum* (**2**) is altogether more exciting, but not always an easy plant, preferring sheltered cool moist soils. The lanky stems reach up to 180cm tall, bearing a profusion of dainty lavender-purple flowers. W. China. Jul.-Aug. ☼ 'Album' - white, 100cm; 'Hewitt's Double' - 90cm, double mauve flowers, very fine.

Monkshoods *Aconitum* HP are Delphinium-like plants, equally fine in gardens and equally poisonous. They are plants for rich moist soils in the semi-shade. *A. napellus* forms stout erect clumps, up to 90cm tall, with shiny green cut leaves and spikes of hooded, deep dull blue, bumblebee flowers. Easy to grow. Europe. Jun.-Aug. ☙ 'Bicolor' - blue and white flowers in branched spikes; 'Bressingham Spire' - deep violet-blue. *A. wilsonii* (**3**) is finer but taller, with exquisite rich dark blue flowers. China. Aug.-Oct. ☙ *A. septentrionale* (**4**) reaches 80cm tall with neat glossy green, but lobed leaves, and spikes of greenish-white hooded flowers. N. Europe. May-Jul. ☙☼ 'Ivorine' - ivory-white flowers, very fine.

1

2

BUTTERCUP FAMILY (contd) **Paeony** HP is one of the most flamboyant and eye-catching of all garden flowers. Paeonies like deep rich soils and greatly resent disturbance of any sort. Most are excellent for cutting. *Paeonia officinalis* (**1**) is the old cottage garden Paeony, forming clumps up to 70cm tall, with huge blowsy blooms in rich satiny crimson shades or pink. Double forms are more generally seen. Europe and W. Asia. June-July. ☼➌△ 'Alba Plena'; 'Rosa Plena'; 'Rubra Plena'. *P. lactiflora* is taller and more erect. The large, sweetly-scented flowers are single or double, white, cream, pink or red. Generally known as 'Chinese Paeonies' these glorious plants are perhaps the most widely grown of all. There are numerous named varieties. E. Asia. May-July. ☼➌△ *P. mlokosewitschii* (**2**) from the Caucasus, is a much sought after plant with its bold grey-green leaves and soft yellow goblet flowers. May. ☼➌

MIGNONETTE FAMILY has only a single species that is grown in our gardens. **Mignonette** *Reseda odorata* (**3**) HA is an old-fashioned annual, grown primarily for its delicious fragrance. Plants grow to 30cm high, with sprawling stems and dense spikes of small whitish flowers. Middle East. Jun.-Aug. ☼

3

1

3

2

ROSE FAMILY is a large cosmopolitan family containing many trees and shrubs as well as herbs. **Geums** HP are a large genus of plants with pinnately-lobed leaves and feathery fruit heads. *Geum quellyon (= G. chiloense)* (**2**) is compact with orange flowers. Chile. Jun.-Jul. ☼☀ Hybridized with the more sprawling *G. coccineum* it has produced the finest garden Geums, mostly 30-40cm tall: 'Copper-tone' - coppery-orange; 'Lady Stratheden' - double, yellow; 'Mrs Bradshaw' (**1**) - double, crimson. *G. borisii* is a neat grower, up to 30cm tall, with intense orange flowers. Jun.-Jul. *G. rivale* (**3**) is the native European Water Avens, a modest plant formerly much cultivated in

4

cottage gardens. May-Jul. *Potentilla atroviolacea* HP has a lax sprawling habit with hand-like, deep green leaves, white-felted beneath, and sprays of dark crimson flowers. Himalaya. Jul.-Oct. ☼ 'Gibson's Scarlet' - the best form. **Goatsbeard** *Aruncus silvester* HP thrives in damp, semi-shaded places. It forms erect tufts, up to 150cm tall, with cut leaves and wide pyramidal plumes of fluffy milky or creamy-white flowers. Europe & W. Asia. Jun.-Jul. ☻ **Lady's Mantle** *Alchemilla mollis* (**4**) HP is a delightful and accommodating plant, forming neat tufts up to 45cm tall, with numerous rounded, lobed leaves, in a soft bluish-green. Sprays of tiny flowers give a yellowish-green haze over a long season. It looks particularly fine by water or in paving. Balkans & Turkey. Jun.-Aug. ☼☻△★

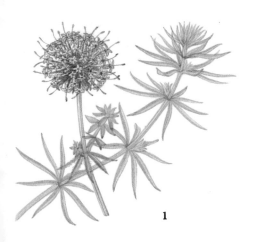

1

MADDER FAMILY is a widespread family of shrubs and herbs, particularly so in the tropics, with paired or whorled leaves and funnel-shaped flowers. **Phuopsis** *Phuopsis stylosa* (**1**)HP is a creeping plant, up to 20cm tall, with sprawling angled stems and distinct whorls of narrow pointed leaves. The bright rose-pink flowers are slender and borne in globular heads. An elegant plant, though rather invasive, forming broad low mats in time, though it prefers a well-drained soil. One drawback is its foxy smell: There is also a white-flowered form. W. Asia. Jun.-Jul. ☼

RUE FAMILY is a family primarily of hot dry countries containing the familiar oranges and lemons (*Citrus*). Few are reliably hardy in our gardens. The following, however, is well worth growing. **Burning Bush** *Dictamnus albus* (= *D. fraxinella*) (**2**) HP is a stout glandular plant, up to 75cm tall, with ash-like leaves. The large flowers are borne in substantial terminal racemes with purplish-pink petals. During hot evenings the plant exudes volatile oils which, it is said, can be ignited without harming the plant. Few can have succeeded in producing this effect, despite the plant's common name. C. & S. Europe. Jun-Aug. 'Alba' - white and equally striking.

2

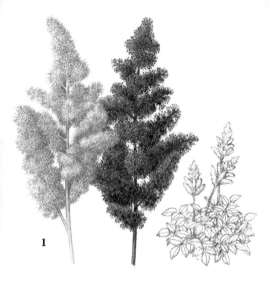

1

SAXIFRAGE FAMILY is a large and diverse family, widely distributed and containing shrubs and herbs, including numerous alpine species. **Astilbes (1)** HP are a popular and charming group of good garden plants for moist sites on good soils. Their origin is complex, involving various Asian species, *Astilbe astilloides*, *A. japonica*, *A. sinensis* and *A. thunbergii*. All form thick erect tufts with green, bronzed or purplish, cut ferny foliage. The plumes of tiny flowers come in shades of pink and red as well as white. Jun.-Aug. ☕ **Bergenias** HP are not

2

everyone's favourite plants, but these adaptable leafy perennials are remarkably good as a contrast to more delicate foliage. They look particularly fine in the shrub border. *Bergenia cordifolia* (**2**) is the commonest, forming a spreading mat of large, rounded, heart-shaped, green leaves. The drooping clusters of pink flowers rise on stems up to 30cm tall. E. USSR. Apr.-May. ☼◐ 'Purpurea' - particularly fine form. *B. ciliata* has broad rounded leaves and sprays of pale pink or white flowers. W. Himalaya. Mar.-Apr. ☼◐ Nurseries sell a range of Bergenias under various cultivar names: 'Abendglut' - rosy red and 'Baby D⌐ - pale pink, are both particularly fine.

1   2

SAXIFRAGE FAMILY (contd) **London Pride** *Saxifraga umbrosa* (**1**) HP is widely grown. It is an elegant plant forming neat rosettes of scalloped leaves with thin stems, up to 30cm high, carrying graceful panicles of small white, pink and yellow spotted, flowers. Pyrenees. May-Jun. ☾● 'Aurea Punctata'- yellow leaf variegations; 'Eliott's Var.' - dwarfer and pinker. **Bridal Wreath** *Francoa sonchifolia* (**2**) HP is a subtle beauty, forming dense leafy tussocks. The slender sprays of flowers rise on 50cm stalks, the petals white with a hint of pink. Chile. Jun.-Jul. ☾ **Heucheras** HP are graceful plants with neat foliage and pretty sprays of small ·wers.

Alumroot *Heuchera sanguinea* is a tufted plant with a tough woody stock and rounded, lobed leaves. The loose panicles of feathery flowers are crimson-scarlet. N. America. Jun.-Sept. ☼☻ Most garden varieties are of hybrid origin involving *H. sanguinea* and *H. americana* (**3**), generally known as *H.* x *brizoides*. 'Bressingham Blaze' - coral red, 30cm; 'Firebird' - deep red, 5cm; 'Gloriana' - rose-crimson, 60cm; 'Oakington Jewel' - bronze-marbled leaves and coral-red flowers, 60cm; 'Red Spangles' (**4**) - crimson-scarlet, 50cm, very fine.

1

2

SAXIFRAGE FAMILY (contd) **Foam Flower** *Tiarella cordifolia* (**2**) HP is a pretty and useful little plant for moist shaded positions. The plants form a low mass of soft-green, heart-shaped, lobed leaves. The white fluffy flower spikes rise on their stems to 25cm tall. N. America. Apr.-Jun. 🌓● *T. wherryi* is similar but the leaves have a dark central zone and the flowers are tinted pink. **Tellima** *Tellima grandiflora* (**1**) HP, also from N. America, is more robust, 60cm high with coarse, rounded, lobed leaves, which bronze in the

3

autumn and greenish, bell-shaped flowers in loose spikes. A subtle beauty. May-Jul. ☺● 'Purpurea' - handsome purple-green foliage. **Kirengeshoma** *Kirengeshoma palmata* (**3**) HHP is a strikingly handsome plant, despite its tongue-twisting name. Athough hardy, the young growths can be caught by frost. Plants form tufts up to 80cm tall, with large maple-like leaves. The yellow flowers are broadly bell-shaped with five wide petals. Well worth growing, it prefers moist places. Japan. Sept.-Nov. ☺

FIGWORT FAMILY is a large and diverse family scattered throughout the world and containing numerous herbs but few woody species. **Cape Figwort** *Phygelius capensis* (**1**) HHP is a semi-woody plant with stems up to 90cm high, often more, with deep green oval leaves. The tubular, red, pendant flowers are borne in loose terminal panicles. Looks particularly fine against a wall. South Africa. Jul.-Oct. ☼☽ *P. aequalis* HP is a finer plant with stronger stems, only 60cm tall, carrying large clusters of buff-rose flowers. South Africa. Jul.-Sept. ☼☽ 'Alba' - delightful creamy-white flowers.

Foxgloves *Digitalis* form a small genus, primarily European in origin. **Common Foxglove** *D. purpurea* (**2**) HB is by far the most well-known, succeeding in moist soils in dappled shade. The flowering stems rise to 150cm, bearing the characteristic drooping tubular flowers in rose-purple, pink or white, spotted within. W. Europe. Jun.-Aug. ☼ 'Excelsior' probably the finest strain. *D. grandiflora* (= *D. ambigua*) (**3**) HP forms rosettes of dark green leathery leaves. The flowers are pale yellow, marked brown, borne in spikes up to 60cm tall. C. & S. Europe. Jun.-Aug. ☼☻ *D.* x *mertonensis* HP is very fine, with its soft grey leaves and flowers the colour of crushed strawberries, 75cm. Jun.-Aug. ☼☻

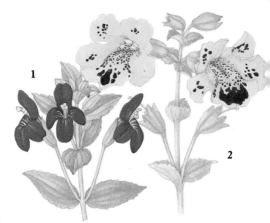

FIGWORT FAMILY (contd) **Monkey Flowers** *Mimulus* are charming and fine flowering plants for cool, moist but sunny places. *M. cardinalis* (**1**) HP is an erect plant growing to 70cm tall, with soft grey stem and leaves. The relatively large flowers are a bright rosy-scarlet. California. Jun.-Sept. ☼❂ *M. ringens* is similar but with pale violet flowers. *M. guttatus* (**2**) HP is a creeping perennial with erect stems to 60cm, pale green foliage and bright yellow flowers, spotted red in the throat. W. North America. Jun.-Sept. ☼❂ There are some fine cultivars such as 'Firedragon' - 15cm, orange-red; 'Harlequin' - 25cm, primrose, red and yellow; 'Ohrid' - 30cm, yellow and maroon; 'Shep' - 25cm, yellow blotched brown.

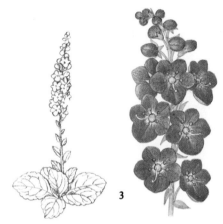

3

Mulleins *Verbascum* is a genus of often stout biennials or perennials, frequently with hoary stems and long spikes or panicles of flowers. **Aaron's Rod** *V. thapsus* HB, native to Britain, and *V. phlomoides* from C. & S. Europe are often seen in old or neglected gardens. *V. phoeniceum* (**3**) HP is up to 90cm tall, with smooth leaves and lax racemes of violet or purplish flowers. E. Europe & W. Asia. May-Aug. ☼ 'Cotswold Queen' - amber-purple; 'Cotswold Gem' - rose (both reliable perennials of hybrid origin involving *V. phoenicum*). *V. olympicum* has handsome silvery-grey, felted leaf-rosettes and silvery spikes of primrose yellow flowers. Greece. Jul.-Aug. ☼ In addition there are some fine cultivars available.

1

FIGWORT FAMILY (contd) **Nemesia** *Nemesia strumosa*
(**1**) HHA are gay, rather jewel-like plants. The small,
pouched flowers are borne in dense racemes in a
dazzling range of colours from white and yellow to
pink, vivid oranges to magenta-purple. These plants
relish a rich, moist soil. South Africa. Jul.-Sept. ☼
Seedsmen offer fine mixtures, such as 'Carnival Mixture' - 20cm; 'Sutton's Large Flowered' - 30cm.
Penstemon is a large American genus of herbs and
subshrubs with opposite pairs of simple leaves and
racemes or panicles of showy tubular foxglove-like
flowers. Most are easily rooted from cuttings but few
are reliable hardy, except in warmer districts. *Penste-*

2   **3**

mon barbatus (= Chelone barbatus) HHP forms erect
clumps, up to 90cm tall, with grassy leaves and
narrow panicles of brilliant scarlet flowers. Very
striking. Mexico. Jul.-Sept. ☼ There are some
free-flowering Penstemon cultivars that are depend-
ably hardy in all but the severest winters. 'Garnet' (**3**)
- 60cm, deep red; 'King George' - 80cm, salmon-red
with a white throat; 'Pink Endurance' - 60cm, clear
pink; 'Sour Grapes' (**2**) - pale purplish-rose, very
appealing, but perhaps less hardy, especially when
young.

1

Figwort Family (Penstemons contd) *Penstemon heterophyllus* HHP is an erect subshrub, up to 100cm tall, though often less, with whorls of slender leaves and racemes of blue, purple or lavender flowers. California. Jul.-Sept. ☼ 'True Blue' - the finest cultivar. *P. hybridus* (**1**) HHP is a plant of mixed origin, but with *P. cobaea* and *P. gentianoides* in its parentage. Most are rather erect perennials with serrated, lance-shaped leaves and large, drooping flowers in scarlets, pinks, lavenders, purples and whites, often prettily marked. They are often grown as half-hardy annuals. Various mixtures are offered in seed catalogues.

2

Snapdragon *Antirrhinum majus* (**2**) HP (though generally grown as an annual) is one of the most widely grown and most popular bedding plants. They succeed best on rather poor, well-drained soils. Modern strains come in a wide range of colours, except blue. Some forms are resistant to the dreaded Antirrhinum Rust, which can ruin plants, and these should be grown if rust is prevalent in the district. S. Europe. Jul.-Oct. ☼☽ 'Tom Thumb' - 15cm. a good dwarf strain, as are 'Little Gem' and 'Pixie'. Others include 'Coronette Mixed' - 40cm; 'Madame Butterfly' - 90cm; 'Sutton's Triumph Special Mixture' - 45cm, very fine.

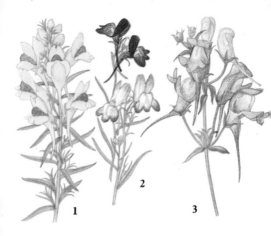

1   **2**   **3**

FIGWORT FAMILY (cont) **Toadflaxes** *Linaria* are small snapdragon-like flowers with a long spur, mostly Mediterranean in distribution. *L. vulgaris* (**1**) HP is a rampant plant, up to 50cm tall, with slender grey-green foliage and yellow and orange flowers. Europe. Jul.-Oct. ☼ *L. maroccana* (**2**) HA is the most widely grown, with slender erect stems to 40cm, grey-green foliage and racemes of purple, crimson, pink, blue or white flowers. N. Africa. Jun.-Aug. ☼ Many of the named varieties, such as 'Fairy Bouquet', are hybrids with *L. bipartita* and *L. reticulata*. **Parrot Flower** *L. triornithophora* (**3**) HHP is the cream of the toadflaxes, 90cm tall with oval grey-green leaves. The relatively large flowers are purplish with yellow mouths and the

4

5

spurs point downwards like a parrot's tail. Not always easy to grow, it needs a sheltered site. Spain & Portugal. Jul.-Oct. ☼ **Speedwells** *Veronica* HP are annual or perennial herbs with paired leaves and pretty four-petalled flowers, often blue or pink. *V. spicata* (**5**) has a creeping stock and stems up to 30cm tall bearing oblong leaves amd dense spikes of violet-blue flowers. Europe & Asia. Jun.-Jul. ☼☻ 'Barcarolle' - rose-pink, 45cm; 'Blue-fox' - lavender blue, 40cm; 'Red-fox' - deep red, 35cm. *V. teucrium* (**4**) forms neat tufts 20-30cm tall with oval, serrated leaves and bright blue flowers. Europe. Jun.-Aug. ☼☻ 'Royal Blue'; 'Shirley Blue'; 'True Blue'; 'Treharne' - golden-green leaves and deep blue flowers, 20cm, very effective.

1

POTATO FAMILY is a large and economically important family, primarily tropical in distribution. **Chinese Lantern** *Physalis alkekengi* (including *P. franchetii*) (**1**) HHP is a robust, spreading, often invasive plant with thin erect stems, 30-80cm tall, bearing small inconspicuous white flowers. The fruits are very colourful, with their enlarged, papery, bright orange-red calyx. Ideal for drying. Europe & Asia. Jul.-Oct. ☼☀★△ 'Giant Scarlet' - the best form. **Salpiglossis** *Salpiglossis sinuata* (**2**) HHA is an erect sticky plant, up to 70cm tall, with

2   **3**

oblong, lobed leaves. The relatively large, funnel-shaped flowers range in colour from rich scarlets and violets to blue, pink, yellow and white, though often multi-coloured and jewelled with a network of conspicuous veins inside. An exotic-looking plant for warm sheltered sites. Chile. Jul.-Sept. ☼☀ 'Splash' - 45cm, one of the best mixtures. **Nierembergia** *Nierembergia hippomanica* (**3**) HHA is a neat bushy plant with funnel-shaped, violet-blue flowers, borne in great profusion. The usual plant grown is var. *violacea*. Argentina. Jul.-Sept. ☼

219

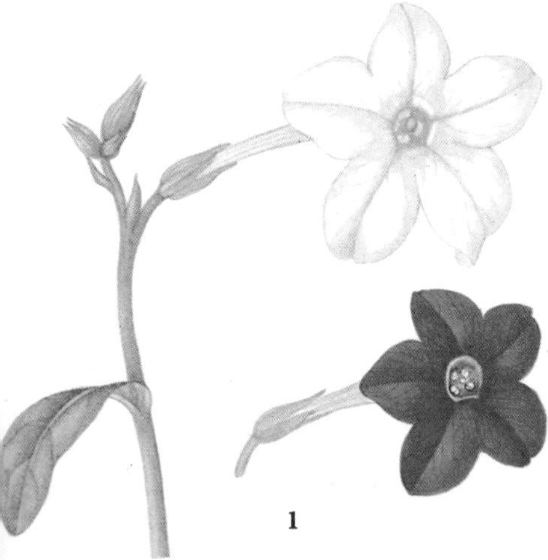

1

POTATO FAMILY (contd) **Sweet Tobacco** *Nicotiana alata* (**1**) HHA is strictly a perennial, overwintering in the mildest districts. The fragrant, white flowers open in the evening or during dull weather. Best in warm sheltered sites. S. America. Jul.-Sept. ☼◒ *N.* x *sanderae* is a hybrid between *N. alata* and red-flowered *N. forgetiana*. White to pink, lilac, rich wine-red and even lime-green forms range in height from 45 to 75cm. Their flowers lack the strong fragrance of *N. alata* but open in all but very bright weather. **Petunia** *Petunia* x

2

hybrida (**2**) HHA is one of the most popular and showy of all summer bedding plants. The plants grown in gardens are hybrids between two South American species, *P. axillaris* and *P. integrifolia*, erect or sprawling in habit, up to 60cm tall. The large funnel-shaped flowers are rather floppy, in a gaudy array of colours. There are compact forms as well as those with frilled petals - and some extremely nasty fully double cultivars, with bloated blooms. Seedsmen offer a wide range of cultivars. Jun.-Sept. ☼

1

MIRABILIS FAMILY **Marvel of Peru** *Mirabilis jalapa* (**1**) HHP has become a popular garden plant in recent years. Though superficially resembling a *Petunia* it is a member of a distinct tropical family. The tuberous roots can be lifted and treated like Dahlias. The plant grows to about 60cm high, with rather pale oval leaves. The striking trumpet flowers come in a range of colours from crimson and purple to pink, yellow and white. Flowers are borne in succession over a long season. Tropical America. Jul.-Oct.

NASTURTIUM FAMILY is a small family, primarily South American in origin. **Nasturtium** *Tropaeolum majus* (**2**) HHA is a vigorous trailing or climbing plant with rounded parasol leaves and succulent stems. The relatively large flowers are often in bright shades of yellow, red or orange. It will succeed on most average soils, but spray against blackfly. S. America. Jul.-Oct. ☼ 'Spitfire' - trailing with cream and white, speckled and blotched leaves and fiery red flowers. The dwarf 'Tom Thumb' strains are crossed with another, non-climbing species, *T. minus*.

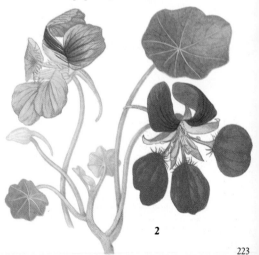

2

NASTURTIUM FAMILY (contd) **Chilean Flame Flower**
Tropaeolum speciosum (**1**) HP, though not always easy to
grow, is a most spectacular climber, up to 2-3m. The
pretty leaves are a fine foil to the brilliant scarlet
flowers. It needs a cool moist soil. Chile. Jul.-Aug. ☼
Canary Creeper *T. peregrinum* (**2**) HHA is a vigorous
pale green climber, up to 3m tall, with canary-bird
flowers. Peru. Jul.-Sept. ☼☻ *T. tuberosum* HHP has
small, oblong, potato-like tubers just below the soil
surface. The stems climb to 3m or more, bearing small
scarlet and orange-yellow 'Nasturtium' flowers. S.
America. Jul.-Oct. ☼☻

CARROT FAMILY is a large and complex family of mostly annual and perennial herbs, worldwide in distribution. **Masterwort** *Astrantia majus* (**3**) HP is a robust plant, up to 90cm tall, with circular, lobed leaves. The flower-heads are like small pincushions surrounded by a whorl of narrow, whitish or pinkish bracts. All Masterworts thrive in cool, moist, semi-shaded places. C. Europe & W. Asia. Jun.-Aug. ☘ **Sea Hollies** *Eryngium* HP are striking, often spiny plants, useful as focal points in mixed borders. *E. bourgatii* (**4**) HP, dwarfer, up to 45cm, has blue-green leaves striped white and spiny metallic-blue flowerheads. Pyrenees & Spain. Jul.-Aug. ☼★

CARROT FAMILY Sea Hollies (contd) **Miss Willmott's Ghost** *E. giganteum* HB is the finest of all, 1m tall with oblong green leaves. The thistle-like whitish flower-heads are surrounded by spiny bracts, suffused with silver and metallic blue. W. Asia. Jul.-Sept. ☼★ *E. alpinum* (**1**) HP has a much -softer look with longer flowerheads surrounded by feathery, softly spiny, blue bracts. 75cm tall. C. Europe. Jun.-Aug. ☼★ *E. variifolium* HP is 60cm tall with marbled, evergreen leaves and small bluish-white flowerheads. Europe or W. Asia. Jul.-Sept. ☼ *E. amethystinum* (**2**) and *E. tripartitum*, both HP with numerous small metallic-blue flowerheads, also well worth growing. Jun.-Aug. ☼★

Valerian Family is a reasonably large family distributed throughout the world. Only one species, however, is widely grown. **Red Valerian** *Centranthus ruber* (= *Valeriana ruber*) (**3**) HP is a rather fleshy plant, often seen on walls in milder districts and on sea cliffs in its native region. The stiff stems rise to 75cm bearing pairs of oval blue-green leaves. The small red, pink or white flowers are borne in large misty-looking panicles. An attractive, though often invasive plant, seeding itself about freely once established. The best coloured forms are worth seeking out and propagating by division of the rootstock. Mediterranean. Jun.-Aug. ☼◑△

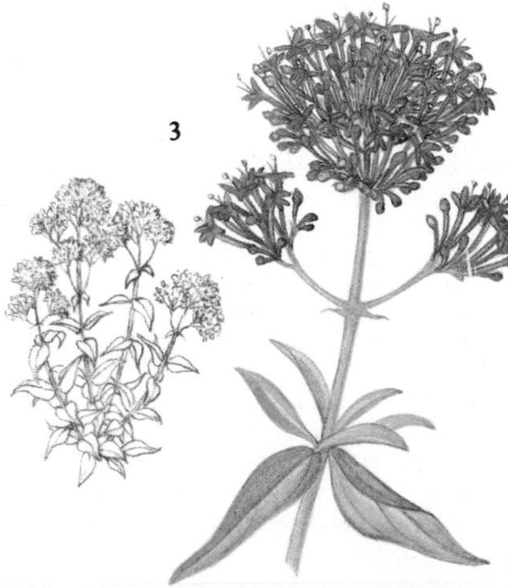

3

1

VERBENA FAMILY is a large and primarily tropical family, closely related to the Mint Family but with many woody trees and shrubs. **Vervain** *Verbena patagonica* H-HHP is an erect, square-stemmed plant, 75-100cm tall, with narrow lance-shaped leaves. The small violet-purple flowers are borne in dense branched spikes forming a broad flattish mass. Good in herbaceous borders, it can be grown as an HHA. Temperate and tropical America. July-Sept. ☼❂△ *V.* x *hybrida* (**1**) HHP is of complex origin and perhaps best treated as a HHA. Plants form untidy, erect to sprawling mats with greyish foliage. The pale pink to deep crimson flowers are borne in small, flat-topped clusters throughout the summer months. Jul.-Oct. ☼❂

PANSY AND VIOLET FAMILY is a popular family known in gardens primarily for the Pansy. **Garden Pansies (2)** HA have been derived from complex crosses between *Viola lutea* and *V. tricolor*. Nurserymen offer a great range of seed or plants in single or mixed colours. *Viola cornuta* HP is the Alpine Pansy, with creeping stems and elegant long-spurred flowers in mauve, pink, purple or white. Pyrenees. May-Sept. ☀☻ 'Boughton Blue' - clear blue. Other Pansies: 'Andross Gem' - pale blue, flushed gold; 'Arkwright's Ruby' - large maroon flowers; 'Bowles' Black' - deep blue-black; 'Irish Molly' - curious mixture of yellow, green and maroon; 'Jackanapes' - red-brown and bright yellow; 'Nora Leigh' - pale violet-blue, very pretty; 'Prince Henry' - deep purple with violet, an old favourite.

2

PANSY AND VIOLET FAMILY (contd) **Wild Pansy** *Viola tricolor* (**2**) HA, with its three-coloured flowers, is frequently grown in gardens. Europe. May-Oct. **Violets** include many species, but relatively few are grown in gardens. Most succeed in moist soils in partial shade. **Sweet Violet** *V. odorata* (**1**) HP is a British native species with heart-shaped leaves and long runners, forming a mat of green eventually. The flowers are deep violet-blue and sweetly scented in the best forms. Many of the old-fashioned varieties, both single and double forms, in various shades of blue, violet, pink or white, were difficult to maintain in cultivation and unfortunately have been replaced by 'Governor Herrick', the florists' violet, which is boring and unscented. Europe. Mar.-May. ☀

3

GINGER FAMILY is a fairly large, primarily tropical family, with showy, often thin-petalled flowers. **Canna Lily** or **Indian Shot** *Canna indica* (**3**) HHP is a popular and bold plant for summer bedding schemes, much used in the tropics, but outdoors in temperate regions suitable only for warm sunny districts. Plants grow up to 1.5m tall, with oblong green or bronzed leaves. The large showy flowers, yellow, orange, red or bi-coloured, occur in short dense spikes. Prefers a moist rich soil. The roots should be wintered in a frost-free place. S. America. Jul.-Sept. ☼

Index of Common Names

Index of Scientific Names

Synonyms are printed in roman *type.*

235

237